Your 20 to Maximizing Retirement Efficiency

FOR THE PURPOSE-BASED RETIREMENT

Casey Weade, CFP®, CLU®, RICP®

Howard Bailey Financial™

Casey Weade/Howard Bailey Financial™
6526 West Jefferson Blvd.
Fort Wayne, IN 46804
www.HowardBailey.com

Book layout ©2013 BookDesignTemplates.com.

Ordering information:
For details, contact the publisher at the address above.

Your 2019 Guide to Maximizing Retirement Efficiency / Casey Weade. —1st ed.
ISBN 9781793861887

Contents

Introduction

Welcome to 2019! Let's look ahead at what the year 2019 will bring: Maybe it is the year you retire. Or, maybe it is the year you start thinking about retirement. Getting your ducks in a row, so to speak. Beginning the planning process. In any case, this year is all about optimizing your financial life and unleashing the efficiency that will be required for a long period of unemployment — which is essentially what retirement comes down to.

If you read my first book, "The Purpose-Based Retirement," you know what I mean by the phrase, "purpose-based." As opposed to what? A non-purposed-based retirement? Exactly!

Unfortunately, what most people do is simply invest and hope for the best with no real strategy. Strategy in retirement planning is like the tracks of a railroad — it keeps you on track to your destination. A "purpose-based" retirement starts at the end and works backwards. Do you want to have enough resources to last throughout your retirement without the worry of running out of money? Of course you do. The idea of running out of money after ten years of retirement is totally unacceptable! And yet, some set themselves up for that very possibility by failing to put in place a purpose-based strategy.

As of the writing of this text, many federal agencies haven't yet released their guidelines for taxes or health care in 2019 — many of which may well change by halfway through the year, anyway, despite initial projections. Regardless of the numbers and projections, though, the most important takeaways, and the explicit aim of this book, are the insights into strategies that can help you make more of your assets in retirement, strategies other financial professionals may not have ever shared with you.

While tax tables fluctuate from year to year and political administration to political administration, these concepts of constant vigilance and retirement efficiency may help you build a legacy or lifestyle that endures. I also hope to impress upon you that, at the pace the retirement landscape changes in the environment we're in today, it is particularly important to sit down with a professional to implement these strategies.

Simply investing and hoping for the best is not a strategy. Without a strategy, you run the risk of having your retirement derailed by severe inefficiencies for a number of reasons. In this book, we will review actions you can take THIS YEAR to improve the efficiency of your financial life.

CHAPTER 1

The Wisdom of Using Multiple Investment Vehicles

T he axiom, "don't put all of your eggs in one basket," certainly applies when it comes to investing. In a volatile and unpredictable market, throwing everything into one investment vehicle and hoping for the best is a recipe for financial ruin. To realize true efficiency in your financial life, it is essential to isolate each *area of purpose* your financial life has.

To illustrate, a sedan with plush upholstery and a state-of-the-art sound system may make for a comfortable road trip. But if you want to haul a load of gravel, it's not the motor vehicle you would choose — you need a dump truck. There are very specific financial vehicles for each goal, or purpose, you have at different times in your life.

Spending emergencies, for example, require liquidity and safety. To offset the effects of inflation, the investment vehicle must have potential for growth. Certain financial vehicles are designed to deal with the contingency of long-term care. Some are best used as a transfer vehicle to maximize your legacy. Others are tax-advantaged. Pounding a square peg into a round hole is futile, so why try to do that with your financial life?

Mutual Funds

There is nothing new about the idea of pooling assets and investing them, which is the essence of a mutual fund. Private investment organizations have been doing that for years, as far back as the eighteenth century. But most of these were closed-end funds — that is, you had to be invited to participate. According to Investopedia.com, the first modern mutual fund was created in 1924 with the creation of Massachusetts Investors' Trust in Boston, Massachusetts. It went public in 1928, and that heralded the beginning of public mutual funds as we know them today. Things were pretty quiet with mutual funds until the 1980s and 1990s when they began racking up double-digit returns, and investors couldn't get enough of them.[1]

Mutual funds can offer a degree of diversification, meaning that splitting assets up into different companies or areas of the market can help mitigate and manage investment risk. The potential problem is that it doesn't guarantee a profit, and it can't protect your principal against losses in a declining market. Mutual funds also offer growth potential for your future. But what they don't offer is protection, predictability, or tax efficiency. I've personally met individuals who relied on mutual funds for *all* of their investment goals. They looked to mutual funds to provide their emergency cash when needed. Mutual funds served as the centerpieces of their income strategies. They depended on mutual funds to hedge against inflation, pay for possible health care expenses, and provide legacies for future generations. Does this not strike you as a commonsense way for your retirement goals to fail? The mutual fund industry has blinded us into thinking we are diversified, when in reality all of your eggs are in one basket.

---

[1] James E. McWhinney. Investopedia. "A Brief History of the Mutual Fund." http://www.investopedia.com/articles/mutualfund/05/mfhistory.asp.

But what happens when those mutual funds lose half their value, as many of them did during the last stock market crash? What happens to your emergency fund when those mutual funds lose half their value? And what if those mutual funds shrink by 50 percent just when you need to tap into them for income to sustain your lifestyle in retirement? What if those mutual funds don't grow fast enough to take care of rising health care costs? What if you leave those mutual funds behind in your individual retirement account (IRA) and Uncle Sam ends up getting the lion's share of the legacy you intended to leave to heirs?

Mutual funds have their place, but they weren't created to solve all your financial problems. Frankly, the same goes for any financial vehicle, be it stocks, bonds, real estate, annuities, private equity, life insurance, cash, etc. I want to make it clear that I have nothing against any of these vehicles, but what I do have a problem with is when we have been brainwashed into thinking just one or two of these vehicles will solve all of our problems.

CHAPTER 2

Let's Talk About Lowering Your Taxes

Your tax return is the heartbeat of your financial life.

Financial planners often spend entirely too much time focusing on investments and neglect the core of every successful person's largest expense — taxes. I often say that if someone can show me how to increase my return by 1 or 2 percent, I will give them a high five, but if they can show me how to cut my tax bill in half I would gladly give them a big wet kiss! Yes, that is a little tongue-in-cheek, but, seriously, think about it — do the math. Also, keep in mind that no financial planner can predict the markets or your returns; it's simply out of their control. However, your year-over-year taxes can be controlled. So, telling me you can make an extra 1 percent sounds great, but showing me exactly how you are going to reduce my tax bill lends much greater confidence.

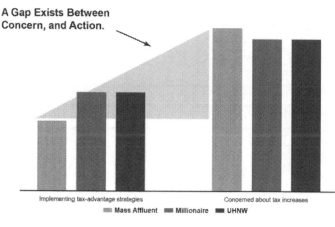

A Gap Exists Between Concern, and Action.

Implementing tax-advantage strategies   Concerned about tax increases

▓ Mass Affluent   ▓ Millionaire   ▓ UHNW

Source: Spectrum Group/Vanguard: "Today's affluent investors: insights and opportunities", 2013

The preceding chart illustrates that, while many, many Americans in different economic classes are concerned about the impact of tax increases, few act on their concerns. The statistics from this chart were drawn up in 2013, but I believe they are still relevant. After all, do you think we collectively are much more likely to act on our concerns six years later?

Unfortunately, the average financial planner hasn't had any formal training in tax planning. As someone who has been educated as a CERTIFIED FINANCIAL PLANNER™ professional, or CFP® professional, and Retirement Income Certified Professional (RICP®), I have had formal training in tax planning. Not to say I am a Certified Public Accountant and prepare tax returns, because I don't. My expertise is not in looking backward and determining what you need to pay the Internal Revenue Service for last year. Instead, my training is in looking forward and helping clients manage their future tax bills by managing today's tax laws.

The Evolution of Tax Laws

Tax laws are constantly changing and shifting.

Sometimes clients will ask me about the one-time capital gains exclusion for people over age fifty-five selling a home. They probably heard about it decades ago, and thought it still existed. Well, sorry to be the bearer of bad news, folks, but that little tax break has gone the way of the rotary dial telephone.[2]

Here's another one. With the Affordable Care Act, or Obamacare, if you didn't have health insurance in 2014, and you didn't qualify for an exception to the penalty, you paid a pretty light penalty of $95 or 1 percent of household income, whichever was greater.[3] Many young taxpayers scoffed at such a slap-on-the-wrist fine and went their merry way, opting to do without insurance. Then, with media outlets buzzing, the 2017 tax law changes were reported to have ended the individual insurance mandate, so it came as a shock to some that, for those who forewent health care coverage in 2018, Uncle Sam still wanted them to pay $695, or 2.5 percent of household income, whichever is higher on their 2018 tax bill.[4] However, in 2019, these fees no longer apply.[5] One thing to keep in mind, though: If the 2017 tax changes sunset as they are scheduled to, we may see a return of the Affordable Care Act tax penalties for the uninsured if Congress doesn't take further action.

---

[2] Investopedia. "Over-55 Home Sale Exemption." http://www.investopedia.com/terms/o/over-55-home-sale-exemption.asp.

[3] Sally Herigstad. Tax Act Professional. "2015 Tax Law Changes and Extensions that Affect Your Clients." https://www.taxact.com/professional/resources/articles/2015-tax-law-changes-that-affect-your-clients/.

[4] Elizabeth O'Brien. Time. Dec. 2, 2017. "The Senate's Tax Bill Eliminates the Individual Mandate for Health Insurance. Here's What You Need to Know." http://time.com/money/5043622/gop-tax-reform-bill-individual-mandate/.

[5] Healthcare.gov. 2018. "No Health Insurance? See if You Owe a Fee." https://www.healthcare.gov/fees/fee-for-not-being-covered/.

Those are just two of hundreds of examples of how tax laws can change. Let's face it — it's Uncle Sam's ball game, and he can change the rules whenever he sees fit. A competent financial planner will be constantly updating his knowledge of how changing tax laws affect his clients. How they have their assets positioned one year may not be a workable strategy the next.

Avoiding Unnecessary Taxes

It's important to recognize that we are discussing tax planning here, not tax evasion. There's an old joke floating around that goes

Q: What is the difference between tax avoidance and tax evasion?

A: Ten to twenty years.

Paying our taxes is what keeps the country running. I may not agree in every respect with how our tax dollars are used, but I pay my fair share of taxes because, as much as we may find writing the check discomforting, taxes are an absolute necessity. If you are like most people, you are a patriotic citizen who wants to pay your fair share — you just don't want to pay a penny more, or pay someone else's fair share. And I don't blame you.

The Internal Revenue Service tax code is a complex document (and getting more complex every year) with more than 4,000,000 words. To put that in some perspective, the "Authorized King James Bible" has only 783,137 words. Leo Tolstoy's "War and Peace," the quintessential long book, has a mere 560,000 words. And nowhere in the IRS tax code will you find a paragraph that proclaims you a more patriotic citizen if you pay more money to Uncle Sam than you are obligated to pay. In fact, I would personally argue that to do so would be doing the economy more harm than good.

Something else you won't find in the tax code: Headings in big, bold type that say, "LOOPHOLES," or "TAX BREAKS." Please don't get me wrong. There are plenty of provisions placed in the code by the government that will help you avoid paying unnecessary taxes, but they just aren't advertised as such. But neither are they buried. You could say they are hidden in plain sight, and quite visible to the educated eye. Knowing where these provisions are and understanding how they affect you *should not be your responsibility*. That is the job of your financial planner, and perhaps your accountant.

Unfortunately, accountants have been trained more in looking backward than forward. You end up sometimes spending a dollar to save fifty cents. A case in point is that of IRA contributions. You can make IRA contributions to reduce your tax bill today, but you are setting yourself up to pay even more taxes down the road. It is the job of your financial planner to work with your accountant to assist in true tax *planning* — looking forward to what's down the road, not just in the rearview mirror.

Complicated by Design?

Is the U.S. tax system complicated by design? I'm not going to go that far. I think it is complicated by default. In other words, Congress passes sweeping legislation, and leaves it to the bureaucrats to hammer out the details, and after that their underlings have no incentive to make things easy to understand.

Answer me this: If there is an easy way to do something and a hard way, which way do you think the government usually choses? That is what my wife would call a "rhetorical question" — one which answers itself and needs no reply.

One reason for the confusion in the tax system is the government uses it not just to raise revenue but to influence social policy, commerce, and the economy. That is why, although everyone agrees the tax code is too complicated, it gets more, not less, complicated every year. Uncle Sam uses it as a carrot-and-stick motivation to accomplish multiple societal objectives.

In a utopian world, taxes would be simple and fair, but that seems to be a hard cocktail for lawmakers to mix. What about a simple, fixed-dollar head tax? Sounds nice, but that would leave the poor paying more than the rich. What about a flat percentage of a person's income without deductions or exemptions? Say 10 percent? It sounds like a good idea on the surface, but then the questions arise. "But I have eight kids; why should I have to pay as much as someone without such family obligations?"

You can see where this is heading, can't you? There is no easy answer. So, for the time being at least, we are stuck with what we have. Instead of launching a charge at the windmills, I have made the following professional decision: I will leave wrangling about tax laws to the politicians. I choose to work within the system we have and make it my business to know all the nuances associated with the current tax code, especially those provisions that can help my clients avoid paying more than their fair share of taxes. In my opinion, this is the very best way I can serve my clients at this time. If change comes, and fair simplification comes to pass, I'll toss my hat into the air along with the rest of you. But, for the time being, let's roll up our sleeves and do a little tax planning with what we have.

What do you mean by that, Casey?

Well, pay close attention to what comes next — just a few ideas to get your engine started.

CHAPTER 3

Perfectly Legal Tax Reduction Techniques Approved and Designed by the IRS

As mentioned in the preceding chapter, Uncle Sam makes the tax rules. He creates the maze, but then is kind enough to give us a map to it so we can maneuver through it. Amongst the 4,000,000-some words in the tax code are several provisions that save us thousands of dollars in unnecessary taxes. They won't jump out at you. You have to know where to look to find them. Take for example, taxes on Social Security.

Taxes on Social Security

In 1935, when the Social Security Act was signed into law by then president Franklin D. Roosevelt, he was reportedly asked if he would tax Social Security benefits. What a ridiculous idea, right? You contribute your own money from your paycheck into the fund all of your working life, and then, when you begin drawing it out, you are taxed on it? As the story goes, FDR was so incensed at the ridiculousness of such a proposal that he pounded his fist on the

Oval Office desk and vowed that he would never tax Social Security benefits. There is some debate as to whether the thirty-second president ever made such a vow. Whether he did or not, the fact remains that Security benefits were not taxed during his lifetime. In fact, the White House was subsequently occupied by seven more presidents before the idea of taxing Social Security benefits came up again. Then in 1982, with the Social Security system in no small degree of fiscal trouble, President Ronald Regan and the leaders of the House and Senate appointed a 15-member National Committee on Social Security Reform. That led to the Social Security Amendments of 1983, a law that said if your base annual income was $25,000 as a single taxpayer, or $32,000 for a married couple filing jointly, then up to 50 percent of your Social Security income would be treated as taxable income.

Bill Clinton was president in 1993 when Congress passed legislation that raised the taxation rate to 85 percent of benefits for single beneficiaries with incomes over $34,000, and couples over $44,000. These threshold amounts were set in 1983 and 1993. Since then, Social Security benefits and general income have increased while these thresholds have remained constant. So they are likely to either remain in place or be raised. It is doubtful that they will be reduced or eliminated.[6]

I know some people are surprised when they get to this intersection of their lives and learn the hard way that some of their Social Security income is taxable. That $30,000 check from Uncle Sam you receive can be the same size as that of your next-door neighbor, but depending on where your other income comes from, you could pay taxes your neighbor wouldn't pay, even if your neighbor has a much larger net worth, or even a higher income. So, let's talk about some things that trigger taxes on your Social Security.

---

[6] Social Security. 2018. https://www.ssa.gov/planners/taxes.html.

Taxes on Social Security

Provisional Income = Adjusted Gross Income + Tax-Free Interest + 1/2 Social Security Income		
If your provisional income is...		**Then your Social Security tax will be...**
Single/Head of Household	*Married filing jointly*	
$0-$25,000	$0-$32,000	0%
$25,000-$34,000	$32,000-$44,000	Up to 50%
$34,000+	$44,000+	Up to 85%

Reportable vs. Non-Reportable Income

Taxes on Social Security benefits depend on how much of your income is reportable and how much of it is not reportable.

Before you go off the deep end here, and think I am in any way suggesting you hide income from the federal government, let me explain the difference in the two categories.

What is *reportable*?

CDs, for one. Many of the families we work with have money at the bank, and that money is often invested in certificates of deposit because they feel it is a safe place for their cash. Why? CDs aren't exposed to the stock market, for one thing. And the idea of a bank holding their money lends a sense of security to them. The bank pays interest on these CDs, of course, but most don't take the interest. They just let it roll back or they reinvest in the CD. Then, at the end of the year, what happens? That interest is reported to the IRS, and is declared on your tax return as income, ***even if the money never passed through your hands.*** At the end of the year you have to declare that as income on your tax return, and what happens is that additional interest income on your tax return goes into a formula that could trigger taxes on your Social Security income.

Mutual funds, index funds, and SMAs — If you have a bond fund, there is interest paid on those bonds. You may be reinvesting that interest, but you still pay tax on that income, just like the income from CDs. When you have a mutual fund, and the fund pays a distribution at the end of the year, what do you do? Most people just buy more shares. Sometimes this happens automatically and you aren't even aware of it until it shows up on your tax return. Once again, you are receiving and being taxed on phantom income that you never saw, but that could potentially trigger a tax on your Social Security income.

Dividends — Here is another big item that could impact the amount you pay in Social Security taxes. Dividends are nice because they are taxed at a lower rate if they are "qualified" dividends. But regardless, they will still show up on your tax return, leading to a potential tax-trigger on your Social Security income.

IRA distributions — This is the area that I see most often causing retirees to pay unnecessary taxes on their Social Security. Nearly every retiree today depends on income from their IRAs to supplement their retirement income. You put those dollars into that account years ago and it resulted in a lower tax bill when you were working. But now that income will result in you potentially having to pay even more taxes.

Interest from municipal bonds — For a long time, municipal bonds have attracted investors because they are income tax free (and sometimes exempt from state taxes, too). But a word of caution here, folks. If you are receiving Social Security benefits, the interest you receive from "muni bonds" may still be included for tax purposes as it counts toward your provisional income.

So, what is *non-reportable?*

Keep in mind, the IRS is using your *adjusted gross income* for its calculations on how much of your Social Security should be taxed, if any. If your modified adjusted gross income, plus one-half of your combined Social Security benefits, plus any tax-exempt interest you receive — called your combined income — exceeds the limits provided by law, then you will be taxed accordingly.

Step 1: Provisional Income	$30,000 in Social Security benefits (1/2=$15,000) + $45,000 in IRA withdrawals
	= $60,000 of provisional income
Step 2: First Threshold	$60,000 of provisional income - $32,000 (first threshold for married filing jointly)
	= $28,000 above first threshold x .5 = $14,000 of taxable benefits
Step 3: Second Threshold	$60,000 of provisional income -$44,000 (second threshold for married filing jointly)
	= $16,000 x .35 = $5,600 of taxable benefits
Step 4: Add 'em up	$14,000 +5,600
	= $19,600
Step 5: Check the Max	.85 x $30,000 (total Social Security benefit) = $25,500
	Compare your results in Step 4 and Step 5. Whichever is lower is your taxable amount.

For illustrative purposes only. Based on 2019 IRS Tax Code.

That means that interest received on tax-deferred or tax-free accounts are ***not reportable*** — that is, the IRS does not consider this ordinary income. Typically, gains paid on annuity balances are tax-deferred and are not required to be listed as income on your 1040 form. The same goes for gains on life insurance balances and Roth IRAs, which are tax-free. Income earned on CDs and gains from non-tax-deferred mutual funds, on the other hand, are reportable, and therefore taxed. That doesn't mean you will never, ever pay taxes on annuity gains. Tax-***deferred*** does not mean tax-***free***. But you won't pay taxes on the money from the annuity until you withdraw it. Meanwhile, that money can be working for you.

Triggering the Tax

This is what happens. The IRS says, "Okay, we're going to add up all your interest, all your dividends, all your tax-free municipal bond interest. We're going to add up all those numbers, plus half of your Social Security income, and all of your other income like pension income, IRA distributions, earned income, and so on. (That is what they call your 'provisional income' or 'combined income.') We're going to add all that up, and if it lands on or surpasses a certain threshold, then you will be subject to Social Security taxes."

The key then is not to pay taxes on interest and dividends if at all possible. Tax-shelter those CDs and mutual funds. Purchase more tax-efficient mutual funds, or switch to index funds, or separately managed accounts. Even better, begin converting your tax-deferred accounts, such as your IRAs,

---

The Tax Torpedo

John and Mary are in the 12% tax bracket, however they just turned 70 ½ and must begin taking required minimum distributions. Their first RMD is $45,000, of which they will have to pay Federal taxes of $5,400 at 12%. Unfortunately, due to this distribution, $20,000 of their Social Security benefits that were previously tax-free will now be taxed, which, at 12%, results in an additional tax due of $2,400. The total taxes paid on their $45,000 distribution is $5,400 + $2,400 = $7,400. This gives them an effective tax rate of 17% on their $45,000 distribution ($7,400/$45,000). The tax torpedo has effectively increased their tax rate by more than 40% (17%-12%=5%/12%).

Note: Hypothetical examples are for illustrative purposes only and are not intended to represent the past or future performance of any specific investment.

to tax-free accounts before you begin drawing Social Security. That way you can reduce your taxes all together.[7] Does it make sense for you to move a portion of the money you currently have sitting in a CD earning minimal interest, or money you have invested in equities, over into an account where the tax on the gains are deferred or even nonexistent? Maybe. Get some professional advice first, though. To quote one of my favorite scriptures:

> "Plans fail when there is no counsel, but with many advisers they succeed." — Proverbs 15:22 (HCSB)

With tax reform in place you may think the tax torpedo has a reduced impact on your finances as a retiree and while marginal tax rates have been reduced it has been cited that retirees still face significant head winds. This excerpt from a 2018 article in the Journal of Financial Planning might just blow your mind:

> Many middle-income retirees can have a federal-alone marginal tax rate of 40.7 percent in 2018. If we return to the 2017 tax brackets in 2026, as called for in the Tax Cuts and Jobs Act, then many middle-income retirees will face a federal marginal tax rate of 46.25 percent.[8]

One of the mottos I stress to all of the families we work with, and one of the axioms I try to live by myself is:
"NEVER spend money on money you're not spending."

---

[7] Pursuant to requirements imposed by the Internal Revenue Service, any tax advice contained in this communication (including any attachments) is not intended to be used, and cannot be used, for purposes of avoiding penalties imposed under the United States Internal Revenue Code or promoting marketing or recommending to another person tax-related matter. Please contact us if you wish to have formal written advice on this matter.

[8] William Reichenstein and William Meyer. Journal of Financial Planning. 2018. "Understanding the Tax Torpedo and Its Implications for Various Retirees." https://www.onefpa.org/journal/Pages/JUL18-Understanding-the-Tax-Torpedo-and-Its-Implications-for-Various-Retirees.aspx.

CHAPTER 4

Optimizing Your Income Tax Brackets

L et's discuss something I know you are thoroughly used to: traditional income taxes. We are talking about the taxes you pay, either on your earned income or on your pension income, or maybe even on deferred compensation you are being paid by an employer. Or even taxes you pay on IRA distributions. Or stock options you exercise.

If you are over age seventy-and-one-half and you have an IRA or some other tax-qualified account, you are probably receiving required minimum distributions (RMDs). As the term suggests, you are required to take RMDs as ordinary income, whether you want to or not. All of this falls into the area of income taxation[9].

You need to be aware of areas where you can reduce these income taxes **with the full blessing, and even the help, of the IRS, and even (believe it or not) accelerate income into certain tax years.**

---

[9] IRS. 2018. "Retirement Plan and IRA Required Minimum Distributions FAQs." https://www.irs.gov/retirement-plans/retirement-plans-faqs-regarding-required-minimum-distributions

A Little History on Income Taxes

This may come as a surprise to some, but income taxes have not always been a part of the American landscape. Taxes and tariffs have been around since colonial days, but the concept of income taxation originated in 1862 when President Abraham Lincoln signed into law a revenue-raising measure to help pay for the Civil War. Citizens were required to pay a 3 percent tax on incomes between $600 and $10,000. A 5 percent tax was levied on incomes of over $10,000.

The public didn't take too kindly to the idea, and income tax was repealed in 1878. Then, in 1913, the sixteenth Amendment breathed new life into income taxation with the words:

"Congress shall have the power to lay and collect taxes on incomes, from whatever source derived, without apportionment among the several states, and without regard to any census or enumeration."

Congress adopted a 1 percent tax on net personal income of more than $3,000, with a surtax of 6 percent on incomes of more than $500,000, and the first Form 1040 was introduced.[10]

We have come a long way since then. The laws governing income taxes have become more complex over time. I know, it makes some want to shut their eyes and just pay up. But with just a little education, we can often save ourselves thousands of dollars, and in some cases, hundreds of thousands.

---

[10] IRS. "Historical Highlights of the IRS." https://www.irs.gov/uac/historical-highlights-of-the-irs. Accessed Aug. 15, 2016.

How Tax Brackets Are Structured

Your tax brackets are graded or tiered, so even though you might be in the 12 percent tax bracket, you are not paying 12 percent of your income in taxes.

Following is an example.

2019 Estimated Income Tax Brackets[11]			
Rate	Single filers	Married filing jointly	Head of household
10%	$0 to $9,700	$0 to $19,400	$0 to $13,850
12%	$9,701 to $39,475	$19,401 to $78,950	$13,851 to $52,850
22%	$39,476 to $84,200	$78,951 to $168,400	$52,851 to $84,200
24%	$84,201 to $160,725	$168,401 to $321,450	$84,201 to $160,700
32%	$160,726 to $204,100	$321,451 to $408,200	$160,701 to $204,100
35%	$204,101 to $510,301	$408,201 to $612,350	$204,101 to $510,300
37%	$510,301+	$612,351+	$510,301+

Now that you have a better understanding of how tax brackets are structured, I want to give you a little nugget of gold. If you are in the 12 percent tax bracket, you should be using every dime of that tax bracket. For instance, if you are married and filing jointly and you receive $50,000 in taxable income, that leaves you with approximately $27,000 of room in your tax bracket without pushing you into the next highest bracket, which is 22 percent. As of 2018, we are in a historically low tax-rate environment.

---

[11] Amir el-Sibaie. taxfoundation.org. "2019 Tax Brackets." Nov. 28, 2018. https://tax-foundation.org/2019-tax-brackets/

According to economists at Goldman Sachs, for fiscal year 2019, the federal government's budget deficit will be a whopping $985 billion.[12] What does that mean for taxes? It means you will most likely pay more than 12 percent on that income when you take it later in life. There is a good chance that, if you leave the money behind for your heirs, they will be forced to pay higher taxes on it. So that begs the question, why not lock in a favorable tax rate today? Now, we can't just take a distribution from those tax-deferred accounts, because we would then pay taxes on our annual gains, right? Instead, we need to ensure we are *moving* those distributions somewhere they can grow and be *distributed, tax free,* in the future.

To Roth or Not to Roth

When Delaware Sen. William Roth first began promoting the idea of the IRA that would later bear his name, he had no way of knowing what an impact it would have on the finances of American retirees. Life was breathed into the Roth IRA when it was included in the Taxpayer Relief Act of 1997, and since then it has been used by millions of Americans to produce tax-free income. Participants either build it from the ground up by funding it on an ongoing basis, or they convert an existing IRA (or another qualified account) to a Roth.

But when is it a good idea do a Roth conversion? After all, if you convert a pre-tax retirement account to a Roth, you create an immediate tax obligation. Depending on the size of the conversion, you could generate so large of a tax liability that it could end up costing you a great deal and be counter-productive to your wealth

---

[12] Kimberly Amadeo. The Balance. "November 21, 2018. "Current U.S. Federal Budget Deficit." https://www.thebalance.com/current-u-s-federal-budget-deficit-3305783

preservation goals. I'm not saying not to do it; I'm saying be careful and get some advice.

A partial Roth conversion can be done, for example, where you convert just enough to keep from kicking yourself into the highest tax brackets.

You should also make yourself familiar with the term **Roth re-characterization**. According to the IRS, "recharacterization" is a provision that allows you to "undo" or "reverse" a rollover or conversion to a Roth IRA by telling the trustee of the financial institution holding your Roth to simply transfer the amount to a traditional IRA (within a trustee-to-trustee transfer or within the same trustee).[13] This kind of strategic "do over" previously allowed you to fill the bottom tax brackets to the penny (but not a penny over), and then do a partial recharacterization the next year. I say previously because the 2017 tax reforms have ended this provision. Moving forward, in 2019 and beyond, recharacterizations will not be allowed.

Partial Conversions

The thing about partial conversions is they let you spread your tax payments out over several years. Beginning in 2010, Roth conversion income limits were eliminated. Today, anyone who has a qualified retirement account, such as a 401(k), IRA, 403(b), can convert it to a Roth IRA, take the tax hit now, and avoid the taxes in retirement. This helps your efficiency by not only reducing your taxable income in retirement, but by potentially eliminating tax on your Social Security benefits and reducing Medicare premiums. So

---

[13] IRS. "IRA FAQs – Recharacterization of Roth Rollovers and Conversions." https://www.irs.gov/retirement-plans/retirement-plans-faqs-regarding-iras-recharac-terization-of-roth-rollovers-and-conversions.

if an investor just wanted to optimize his or her efficiency in retirement, it may be just the thing.

How much can you convert? All of it or a part of it. It depends on your financial goals in retirement and what your tax exposure is. Just remember whatever amount you convert to a Roth becomes taxable as ordinary income (see section 408A(d) of the Internal Revenue Code).

One of the best chapter-and-verse explanations of this provision (Treasury Regulation 1.408A-5) was published by the Cornell University Law School's Legal Information Institute:[14]

> "Question. Can an IRA owner recharacterize certain contributions (i.e., treat a contribution made to one type of IRA as made to a different type of IRA) for a taxable year?
>
> "Answer. Yes. In accordance with section 408A(d)(6), except as otherwise provided in this section, if an individual makes a contribution to an IRA (the FIRST IRA) for a taxable year and then transfers the contribution (or a portion of the contribution) in a trustee-to-trustee transfer from the trustee of the FIRST IRA to the trustee of another IRA (the SECOND IRA), the individual can elect to treat the contribution as having been made to the SECOND IRA, instead of to the FIRST IRA, for Federal tax purposes. A transfer between the FIRST IRA and the SECOND IRA will not fail to be a trustee-to-trustee transfer merely because both IRAs are maintained by the same trustee. For purposes of section 408A(d)(6), redesignating the FIRST IRA as the SECOND IRA will be treated as a transfer of the entire account balance from the FIRST IRA to the SECOND IRA."

Michael Kitces, who writes financial planning strategies for both consumers and financial advisors, gave the following examples in

---

[14] Legal Information Institute, Cornell University Law School. "26 CFR 1.408A-5 – Recharacterized contributions." https://www.law.cornell.edu/cfr/text/26/1.408A-5.

his December 2015 blog entitled, "Using Systematic Partial Roth IRA Conversions and Recharacterizations to Fill the Lower Tax Bracket Buckets."[15]

Using Roth Conversion and Recharacterization to Perfectly Fill a Tax Bracket

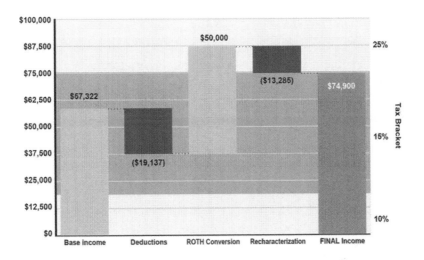

In the first example, a couple has a combined annual income of $60,000 and are considering a Roth conversion for $500,000 in an IRA. Their income places them in the 15 percent tax bracket (2015 income tax rates), and they are aiming to prevent a 28 percent marginal tax rate on their IRA in the future, when their RMDs begin. If they converted the entire account in one year, their combined annual income in that tax year would be $560,000, putting them in

---

[15] Michael Kitces. Nerd's Eye View at Kitces.com. December 2, 2015. "Using Systematic Partial Roth IRA Conversions and Recharacterizations to Fill the Lower Tax Bracket Buckets." https://www.kitces.com/blog/using-systematic-partial-roth-ira-conversions-and-recharacterizations-to-fill-the-lower-tax-bracket-buckets/.

the 39.6 percent tax bracket. A Roth conversion at a 15 percent tax rate to avoid a 28 percent tax rate would have ended up costing them a 39.6 percent tax on their top $100,000! Remember, Kitces was writing this in 2015, so the tax brackets aren't current, but the general principle of filling a bracket still applies today.

Kitces points out that in the preceding scenario, a partial Roth conversion suddenly becomes appealing. Why? Because converting the entire account could drive the couple's marginal tax rate into the top 39.6 percent bracket, which would be so high that they probably would have been better off just leaving the money as a pre-tax IRA and spending it in the future at a lower rate. A partial Roth conversion, on the other hand, allows the couple to create *just enough* income to be subject to the lower tax brackets, while stopping before they reach the upper brackets.

Further, Kitces shows that the couple could convert up to $14,900 while remaining in the 15 percent tax bracket, which topped out at $74,900 for a married couple when the blog was published in 2015. Or, alternately, the couple could still save in taxes by topping out the 25 percent bracket and converting $91,200, while still avoiding the full 28 percent tax bracket, both now and, for the converted dollars, in the future as well.

Kitces makes the point here that the strategy employed in the example above allowed the couple to convert exactly enough to ensure that their IRA would be subject to the lower tax brackets today, but *only* those lower and more favorable tax rates.

Partial Roth Conversions Over Time

What if you are approaching retirement and are in that zone where you have pulled the plug on your paycheck, you have a pre-tax (qualified) IRA account, but you aren't seventy-and-one-half yet, and aren't subject to RMDs? We suggest that a retiree in his or her early sixties, for example, may wish to do a partial Roth conversion *each year throughout their sixties*, so as to whittle down the size of their pre-tax IRA over time.

For instance, let's look at the case of Joyce, a single, sixty-year-old widow. She recently retired with $20,000 a year in Social Security survivorship payments, and a $40,000 per year survivorship pension from her deceased husband's employer. Joyce has $700,000 in an IRA from her own IRA savings as well as her husband's, which she rolled over from his 401(k) upon his death. She also has $200,000 saved in a post-tax brokerage account. In ten years, when Joyce turns seventy-and-one-half, assuming a 7 percent annual growth rate in her IRA, she will face RMDs of more than $50,000 per year. With her Social Security and pension payments, that will push her into the 24 percent tax bracket. By the time she is in her eighties, her RMDs may be more than $100,000 annually, pushing her into a 32 percent tax bracket in her eighties and nineties.

To avoid this scenario, Joyce can affect a Roth conversion. Of course, a one-time Roth conversion — converting all of her $700,000 IRA in a single year — would result in a massive tax. So, instead, Joyce will do a series of small partial conversions, converting $30,000 from her IRA each year for the next ten years — just enough to fill up her 22 percent income tax bracket without pushing her over into a 24 percent tax rate. Year after year, Joyce's small conversions are tapering down her IRA's tax exposure. If she begins this tactic at age sixty, by the time her RMDs begin at seventy-and-one-half, she will still have $900,000 in her IRA thanks to our assumed 7 percent growth, but that will necessitate RMDs of $35,000 — as opposed to the original $50,000 — keeping her within the 22 percent income tax bracket to which she has become accustomed.

In the meantime, Joyce will have accumulated a tax-free Roth IRA, projected to have grown to more than $300,000 by age seventy-and-one-half (assuming she paid her Roth conversion at a 22 percent federal and 3 percent state income tax rate and assuming she reinvests our assumed annual 7 percent market growth). If Joyce was a little more aggressive, she could have filled out the 24 percent tax bracket each year before the age of seventy-and-one-half allowing for a Roth conversion of about $100,000 per year. At that rate, she would have most likely converted 100 percent of her traditional IRA to a Roth IRA by the time she was seventy-and-one-half, resulting in maintaining a 12 percent tax bracket for the rest of her life without ever having to see a required minimum distribution increase her taxes or affect her Medicare premiums. Effectively, she could live every retiree's dream of passing an inheritance tax-free to her heirs. An often-overlooked area of Roth conversion planning is the tax rate of the heirs that will ultimately inherit the assets — they could potentially be in a substantially higher tax bracket than yourself.

Conversions — Tax Cuts and Jobs Act of 2017

I have one more point to make regarding taxes and Roth conversions. Now that you are familiar with the idea of partial Roth conversions over time and the concept of "filling up the bracket," let's talk about those restructured income tax brackets. To refresh, the last several years we have had seven brackets for income taxes: 10, 15, 25, 28, 33, 35 and 39.6 percent. Under the Tax Cuts and Jobs Act of 2017, 2018 and beyond will have brackets of 10, 12, 22, 24, 32, 35, and 37 percent . . . until 2025. That's right — the Act has sunset provisions that sets an expiration date on these bracket settings, making it important that you understand this low tax rate environment won't last forever.

Merging Brackets[16]			
Single Filers			
2017 Rate	*2017 Bracket*	*2018 Rate*	*2018 Bracket*
10%	$0 - $9,325	10%	$0 - $9,525
15%	$9,326 - $37,950	12%	$9,525 - $38,700
25%	$37,951 - $91,900	22%	$38,700 - $82,500
28%	$91,901 - $191,650	24%	$82,500 - $157,500
33%	$190,651 - $416,700	32%	$157,500 - $200,000
35%	$416,701-$418,400	35%	$200,000-$500,000
39.6%	$418,400	37%	$500,000+
Married Filing Jointly			
2017 Rate	*2017 Bracket*	*2018 Rate*	*2018 Bracket*
10%	$0 - $18,650	10%	$0 - $19,050
15%	$18,651 - $75,900	12%	$19,050 - $77,400
25%	$75,901 - $153,100	22%	$77,400 - $165,000
28%	$153,101 - $233,350	24%	$165,000 - $315,000
33%	$233,351 - $416,700	32%	$315,500 - $400,000
35%	$416,701-$470,700	35%	$400,000-$600,000
39.6%	$470,700+	37%	$600,000+

The preceding chart reflects differences in tax brackets between 2017 and 2018. To put this into context with Roth conversions, if your joint income with your spouse for 2019 is in the $168,00-plus range, you can convert about $150,000 (the top of the bracket is $321,450) of traditional IRA funds to a Roth without being pushed out of the 24 percent income bracket. If it was 2017, that same

---

[16] KDP Certified Public Accountants. Feb. 6, 2018. "2017 vs. 2018 Federal Income Tax Brackets." https://www.kdpllp.com/2017-vs-2018-federal-income-tax-brackets/.

$315,000 would have put you in the 33 percent taxation range. That's a pretty big difference in the amount of money you get to keep in your pocket, I'd say. Again, there is a sunset provision in this tax law, so it's important to consider whether you might want to do a Roth conversion before or during retirement, and whether you'd rather do those conversions in a low tax environment or in a higher one.

CHAPTER 5

Making Capital Gains Tax Rules Work for You

Another type of tax is capital gains. We pay these taxes when we sell something and make a profit. Hopefully, this is a long-term capital gain, instead of the type of short-term capital gain that occurs when we sell something we have owned for less than a year at a profit. This type of profit is taxed as ordinary income at your highest marginal tax rate. So, if you buy a share of Apple stock today, and six months from now sell it at a profit, then that will be considered short-term capital gains by the IRS and be taxed as ordinary income. But if you hold it for longer than a year, it is a considered a long-term capital gain, which, for most of us, is taxed at a much lower rate.

There are a few areas where long-term capital gains come into play for our clients. No. 1 could be a stock that you inherited. Let's say your mother or father passes away and you inherit that Apple stock. Let's further say that you inherited it ten years ago when it was worth a lot less money. The ownership date for the purpose of establishing the tax cost of that inheritance becomes the date when you inherited the stock. Now, ten years later, you go to sell the Apple stock. That is considered a long-term capital gains tax. So, you get to add that on a different section of your tax return, and you will be taxed at 0, 15 or 20 percent, depending on how much other taxable income you have for that year. If it were considered as ordinary income, you could be taxed as much as 37 percent. What's nice about inherited stock is that it will always be treated as a "long-term" capital gain, regardless of the holding period.

Can you see how long-term capital gains tax is much more favorable than ordinary income taxes? That is why it's more advantageous to own either individual stocks, or exchange-traded funds, instead of mutual funds, so that you can control your taxation.

A mutual fund is a pass-through entity. When you purchase a share of a publicly traded mutual fund, you are buying a share of an existing company that owns many individual investments, each with its own pre-existing tax liabilities. Whether or not you ever sell those shares, you will be responsible for a proportional share of the existing tax liability. The internal trading activity of the fund manager and fund inflows and outflows affect all shareholders, even though you may have performed no trading for the year. If a fund has assets that have appreciated over time, and they sell them during the current tax year, it could create a situation where a new investor buying shares could inherit the tax liability of existing holdings. For example, an investor purchases ten shares of an equity mutual fund for $10 per share (total investment of $100). Shortly thereafter, the mutual fund passes through a $2 per share short-term capital gain that has built up during the previous twelve months. If we assume that the shareholder simply reinvests all dividends and capital gains, the following chart shows what happens.

Starting Value	$100	10 x $10
Capital Gain	$20	$2 per share
New Share Price	$8	$10 minus the $2 capital gain distribution to shareholders
Capital Gain Reinvested	$20 ÷ $8 per share	2.5 shares purchased
Ending Value	$100	$12.5 x $8

As you can see, you didn't have any gain in real dollars, but you are still stuck with a $20 short-term capital gain distribution taxed at your income tax rate. Had you owned the stock directly, you would have been allowed to defer taxation on the appreciated value of your stock shares, potentially turning a, say, 24 percent tax into a 15 percent tax.

Even worse is the inability to offset net-realized losses during the year against ordinary income. This is just another reason why mutual funds are an inefficient and outdated form of investing.

You may have observed that I noted a potential tax liability of zero percent on your long-term capital gains. We all like not having to pay taxes, so this is a crucial part of your financial education.

2019 Long-Term Capital Gains				
Tax Rate	Single filers	Married filing jointly	Head of Household	Married filing separately
0%	$0 to $39,375	$0 to $78,750	$0 to $52,750	$0 to $39,375
15%	$39,376 to $434,550	$78,751 to $488,850	$52,751 to $488,850	$38,600 to $239,500
20%	Over $434,551	Over $488,851	Over $461,701	Over $244,425

Prior to the 2017 Tax Cuts and Jobs Act tax reform, the 0, 10, and 15 percent tax brackets were based on your income tax bracket. That is no longer. However, the brackets are still stacked in such a way that most people in the 10 to 15 percent income tax brackets won't have to pay tax on long-term capital gains distributions. This may not last forever, so if you have long-term capital gains built up in your investments, now may be a great time to strategically lock in a 0 percent tax rate and increase your tax basis. If you are in a higher tax bracket, you may want to strategically sell your long-term capital gain assets to avoid paying anything higher than 15 percent and potentially avoid the Medicare sur-tax of 3.8 percent.[17,18]

---

[17] Jeff Rose. Forbes. December 5, 2018. "The New 2019 Federal Income Tax Brackets and Rates." https://www.forbes.com/sites/jrose/2018/12/05/tax-brackets-and-rates-2019/#7d3dadd63ec5.

[18] Matthew Frankel. The Motley Fool. December 9, 2018. "Long-Term Capital Gains Tax Rates in 2019." https://www.fool.com/retirement/2018/12/09/long-term-capital-gains-tax-rates-in-2019.aspx.

CHAPTER 6

Reduce Taxes by Getting Control of Your IRA

One of the other ways to reduce your taxes in retirement is to gain control of your IRA, 401(k), and any other retirement plan distributions you may have. What do I mean by getting control? Well, at age seventy-and-one-half, the IRS will force you to begin taking distributions from your qualified retirement plans, such as IRAs, 401(k)s, 457 plans, 403(b) plans, and similar retirement plans. All these plans have one thing in common. You pay no taxes on the money you put into these plans, nor do you pay taxes on the interest you gain while they are growing. But when you begin withdrawing money from them, those withdrawals are considered ordinary income by the IRS and taxed accordingly.

What if you never really need the money from any of these qualified plans? Can you just leave the money there and allow it to continue to grow tax-deferred ad infinitum? No. Uncle Sam has plugged that little loophole with something called RMDs, or required minimum distributions. At age seventy-and-one-half, you will be forced to withdraw a percentage of the balance of these accounts each year, and that percentage gets higher as you age.

The only exception to that is if you are still working for the company with which you have a 401(k).

This presents an interesting opportunity.

Let's say you are working for a company — let's say General Motors — and you are seventy-three years old. You have a 401(k) there, and, let's also say you have other IRAs and retirement accounts. You would rather not have to take money out of those other accounts because you don't need the income right now. But because of your age, the IRS is forcing you to take money out of your other IRAs. You could actually take the money in your other qualified plans and roll it into your 401(k) at the company where you are employed, and not take any RMDs until you quit working.

Now, that isn't necessarily what you should do. You will need to discuss rolling money from one account to another with a financial professional to make sure you are considering any potential fees, limits, or investment options specific to your own situation.

But, there are many techniques like this with which you need to be familiar if you are interested in maximizing your retirement efficiency and minimizing your tax exposure; perfectly legal, perfectly ethical, and perfectly okay with the IRS.

The following table is the table the IRS uses in order to determine your annual required distributions after age seventy-and-one-half. You can see on the table that you simply take the total amount of all your IRAs (the December 31 value of the previous year) and divide by the distribution factor next to your age. That number is the amount of money you have to distribute from those retirement plans.

Someday, you will lose control of those retirement accounts. Losing control in retirement is the last thing a retiree wants. Much of retirement is psychological, and in losing a little bit of control, you lose a little bit of power and a little bit of your freedom in retirement.

IRA Required Minimum Distribution			
Age	Distribution Period	Age	Distribution Period
70	27.4	94	9.1
71	26.5	95	8.6
72	25.6	96	8.1
73	24.7	97	7.6
74	23.8	98	7.1
75	22.9	99	6.7
76	22.0	100	6.3
77	21.2	101	5.9
78	20.3	102	5.5
79	19.5	103	5.2
80	18.7	104	4.9
81	17.9	105	4.5
82	17.1	106	4.2
83	16.3	107	3.9
84	15.5	108	3.7
85	14.8	109	3.4
86	14.1	110	3.1
87	13.4	111	2.9
88	12.7	112	2.6
89	12.0	113	2.4
90	11.4	114	2.1
91	10.8	115+	1.9
92	10.2		
93	9.6		

The key here is to be proactive.

You should begin thinking about ways to gain control of your retirement accounts before you get to age seventy-and-one-half. Let's say you are five years away from age seventy-and-one-half and the government's RMDs. You should be thinking about coming up with a plan to reduce the potential force out of those accounts at age seventy-and-one-half.

For instance, you may say, "Every time my IRA goes up in value, I'm going to start taking a little bit out now so I don't create a bigger problem when I'm seventy-and-one-half, potentially pushing me into a higher tax bracket, or causing more of my Social Security income to become taxable."

What does that mean, specifically?

You may decide to convert money from your traditional tax-deferred retirement accounts to a Roth. This is kind of like "paying it forward." You may have to pay some additional taxes today, but then that Roth IRA is tax-free forever — even after you are gone.

This strategy is especially advantageous if we believe tax rates will be higher in the future. But even if that turns out not to be the case, and tax rates remain the same (not likely, but just for the sake of argument), think about your beneficiaries who may still be working and taking distributions from these accounts decades from today.

Please keep in mind, I said "consider" converting some or all of your retirement accounts to Roth IRAs, I didn't say to go do it. You must sit down with a well-educated, well-rounded financial professional who is literate in these strategies and is able to walk you through the pros and cons of Roth conversion.

Remember, our objective is to protect ourselves against tax events. We may feel certain that taxes will be higher in the future than they are today, but neither you nor I have a crystal ball. We just don't know. But what we can do is control our taxable income every year. This may mean that we project forward what those required distributions will be when you are seventy-and-one-half, and begin strategically converting tax-deferred dollars to Roth. That way, your taxable income won't go through the roof as you age but will remain fairly steady.

Qualified Charitable Distributions

Due to major increases in the standard deduction — from $13,000 for a couple to $24,000 and $6,500 to $12,000 for single filers — many of those who may have historically itemized their deductions in order to capture mortgage interest deductions and charitable contributions (amongst other things) will no longer be able to qualify for those deductions as they will not be larger than their standard deductions. This has presented a major planning opportunity for those interested in putting a few extra bucks back in their pocket in the future.

One of the more obvious options for those who are charitably inclined is to bunch their deductions in order to get over their standard deduction limits. In other words, you may want to set aside the amount you typically give into a separate account, which you can give away as a lump sum in the future. For instance, if you typically tithe $5,000 per year, you may want to set aside $5,000 per year for five years and give $25,000 in a single year, which may also allow you to pick up other deductions you don't typically qualify for, such as mortgage interest and medical expenses.

On the other hand, maybe you don't have the discipline to set aside those funds without spending them for years in lieu of future deductions. In that case, if you are over seventy-and-one-half, you're not yet out of luck, as you may be able to take advantage of rules permitting a qualified charitable distribution, or QCD.

Rules allowing QCDs were originally created under Section 1201 of the Pension Protection Act of 2006, however, they were only effective for two years and lapsed. The rules were reinstated and lapsed several more times until 2015 legislation made the rules permanent. Now, as a result of the Tax Cuts and Jobs Act of 2017, these rules are becoming more popular than ever for retirees.

One benefit of doing a QCD from an IRA is the distribution comes out of the IRA without the tax consequences that would otherwise apply to the withdrawal. Most notably, there is no charitable deduction, but instead there is also no taxable income created in the first place, negating the need to itemize to qualify for the charitable deduction. Through avoiding additional taxable income, you may also be able to avoid additional Social Security taxes or Medicare penalties you would have had if you hadn't contributed directly to the charity.

Here are the rules:

1. You must be at least seventy-and-one-half on the date of distribution.
2. The check must be sent directly to the charity from the IRA custodian.
3. No tax can be withheld from the IRA distribution.

ONE CAVEAT: THE CHECK MUST BE MADE PAYABLE TO THE CHARITY; A CHECK MADE PAYABLE TO THE IRA OWNER THAT IS THEN ENDORSED OVER TO THE CHARITY DOES NOT SATISFY THE QCD REQUIREMENTS.

CHAPTER 7

Watch Your Expenses – Build a Budget

I can't tell you how many retirees I sit down with who have no idea what they are spending on a monthly basis. I would say it is most people.

Let's face it. When you are in retirement, you are on a fixed income. You don't have the luxury of putting in some overtime for a little extra income. Yes, of course, there is the possibility of part-time work, but most employers are looking for younger people to fill those slots. Also, if the work is the least bit physically demanding, your age may exclude you simply because — how can I say it gracefully — you're not a spring chicken anymore. So it's always good regardless of your age to know how much you have coming in and how much you can reasonably afford to spend at any given time, but this is especially the case when you retire. As Bill Earle so succinctly put it: "If your outgo exceeds your income, then your upkeep will be your downfall."

In this age of technology, with so many budgeting tools at our disposal, there is just no excuse for not being able to track our expenses and income. Much of the wonderful software available today is free, too.

Monthly Personal Budget Worksheet

	Estimated Monthly Cost	x12
INCOME		
Income (Draw) From Business	$	$
Income From Other Sources	$	$
TOTAL INCOME	$	$
EXPENSES		
Rent/Mortgage	$	$
Home Insurance	$	$
Health Insurance	$	$
Utilities	$	$
Telephone	$	$
Auto: (payments, gas, repairs)	$	$
Food	$	$
Household Supplies	$	$
Clothing	$	$
Laundry/Dry Cleaning	$	$
Education	$	$
Entertainment	$	$
Travel	$	$
Contributions	$	$
Health	$	$
Home Repair and Maintenance	$	$
Self-Development	$	$
Outstanding Loans and Credit Card Payments	$	$
Miscellaneous Expenses	$	$
TOTAL EXPENSES	$	$
BALANCE (+/–)	$	$

I want you to do a simple exercise with me right now. Ask yourself what you think you spend on a monthly basis. Please write that number down. Next, write down what your gross pay was for 2018. Now, subtract out any pre-tax savings, such as 401(k) or HSA contributions. Have you got that figure? Good. Now, look at those tax brackets I posted earlier, and take out what you would estimate your annual taxes to be. Now, please subtract from that number any after-tax saving you may have done, such as in your taxable brokerage account or savings accounts or Roth contributions. DON'T ignore big purchases such as a new car or home renovation, because I promise you those expenses will return in retirement. THAT is the number you spent last year. Is it bigger than you thought? It always is. Now, start tracking and get prepared.

Creating a Retirement Budget

To create a budget for living in retirement, all you need to do is gather the following:

- Bank statements for the last twelve months
- Total income for the year from all sources
- Tax return from previous year

Using the above materials, make a list of all of your expenses and other financial obligations. You may find it useful to break these down into the following categories:

1. **Absolutely necessary expenses** — food, clothing, transportation, housing, and health care.

2. **Required annual expenses** — insurance premiums, property taxes, auto registrations, etc.

3. **Somewhat essential expenses** — anything for which you receive a bill you could do without but don't want to, such as cable, country club membership, gym membership, subscriptions, etc.

4. **Non-essential expenses** — entertainment, dining out, travel.

Now that you see where your money goes and why, it is simply a matter of prioritizing. You know how much you have coming in, and you know how much you must pay out on the essentials. What's left over can either be saved for posterity or spent having fun.

This may also help you in actually structuring your income strategy for retirement: Separating your **pay checks** from your **play checks**. You may decide you want to guarantee the income necessary to cover certain expenses you decide are essential, while generating income needed for non-essential expenses from at-risk investments. Just food for thought.

CHAPTER 8

Health Care Costs

Health care costs can be daunting, especially if you have been covered under an employer plan for most of your life, but I'm here to tell you, it's okay. You have options once you are retired.

Medicare — Some folks think that, once they qualify for Medicare, they will be covered like a glove for all that ails them. That's not the case. Don't underestimate the cost of Medicare. It's not free. There are four main parts to Medicare — parts A, B, C, and D. You will typically go one of two directions. Either you will sign up for Part A, B, and D, or just Part C, also known as Medicare Advantage.

Medicare Part A is your hospital coverage. As long as you or your spouse have worked for at least ten years, and have paid Medicare taxes, you won't pay a monthly fee or premium for Part A. If you stay overnight in a hospital, or use other Part A services, you will pay a deductible — an amount you must pay before Medicare's coverage kicks in. In 2019, that amount is $1,364.[19] In addition, you may have to pay a copay, depending on your specific type of care.

Medicare Part B covers your doctor visits, tests, and other services. You do have to sign up for Part B, or you will pay a penalty (unless you are covered through an employer or union). The costs

---

[19] Centers for Medicare & Medicaid Services. October 12, 2018. "2019 Medicare Parts A & B Premiums and Deductibles." https://www.cms.gov/newsroom/fact-sheets/2019-medicare-parts-b-premiums-and-deductibles.

for Part B are typically $135.50 annually (2019), unless your taxable annual income is higher than $85,000, in which case Medicare Part B will charge a stepped scale of monthly premium, up to $460.50 for those whose annual incomes are greater than $500,000 (single), $750,000 (married filing jointly) or $415,000 (married filing separate). [20]

This is yet another reason to do a good job with your tax planning. Under Part B, your deductible is $185 per year with a 20 percent copay for most doctors' services after your deductible is met.

Part D is for prescription drug coverage. Premiums for Part D vary, but they are estimated to drop for the second year in a row, to $32.50 a month for 2019. If you have a higher taxable income, you may pay more each month. Again, another reason to do a good job with your tax planning.

Your deductible for Part D will vary from plan to plan, but the maximum is $415 for 2019. After you have paid your deductible, the plan kicks in, and you pay a copay or coinsurance. [21]

Donut Hole — If you spend a lot on medicine, you could have a gap in your drug coverage. At a certain level, your Part D plan may stop paying for your medications altogether. In 2019, that level is $3,820. This is what is often referred to as "hitting the donut hole." While you are in the donut hole, you pay 25 percent of the cost for brand-name prescription drugs. In 2019, you pay 37 percent for ge-

---

[20] Ibid.

[21] David Haass. Forbes. May 16, 2018. "Medicare Part D Prescription Drug Plan Discounts and Highlights for 2019." https://www.forbes.com/sites/forbesfinancecouncil/2018/05/16/medicare-part-d-prescription-drug-plan-discounts-and-highlights-for-2019/#7f110f816819

neric prescription drugs. That percentage has been steadily decreasing and will stop at the year 2020. By then, it will have reached 25 percent. [22]

At some point, you will reach an annual out-of-pocket threshold, which is $5,100 for 2019.[23] Then Medicare will start paying again, and you will have a small copay, or coinsurance, toward your prescription drug costs for the rest of the year. This is where Medigap or Medicare supplement policies come in. This is supplemental insurance provided by private insurance companies that cover some of the gaps traditional Medicare won't cover, such as copays or deductibles. Premiums for this private coverage can vary widely by carrier and state, but expect to pay $100 to $200 per month for a Medigap or Med-Sup policy.

Medicare Advantage Plans — An alternative to traditional Medicare is something called Medicare Advantage, also known as Part C. These plans are sold by insurance companies under the watchful eye of the CMS, or Centers for Medicare and Medicaid Services, typically including Part A, Part B, and Part C under one plan. To qualify, you will have to sign up for Parts A and B, so that means you will at least have to pay the Part B premium on top of your monthly premium for your Medicare Advantage plan itself. These prices vary so widely, I hesitate to quote any average at all.

The bottom line of this exercise is that Medicare *isn't free* and you will have some monthly expenses to deal with, and that Medicare also doesn't cover everything. Eyeglasses, hearing aids, vision care, non-prescription drugs, and dental care aren't covered under Medicare. Probably the most significant of the health needs not covered under Medicare is an extended nursing home stay. You

---

[22] Medicare.com. 2018. "What Kind of Discount Can We Expect in the Medicare Part D Donut Hole or Coverage Gap? https://q1medicare.com/q1group/MedicareAdvantagePartDQA/FAQ.php?faq=What-kind-of-discount-can-we-expect-in-the-Medicare-Part-D-Donut-Hole-or-Coverage-Gap-&faq_id=470&category_id=129.

[23] Medicare.com. 2018. "2019-2006 Medicare Part D Standard Benefit Model Plan Parameters." https://q1medicare.com/PartD-The-MedicarePartDOutlookAllYears.php.

have to figure out how to care for those things out of your own pocket.

On health care costs ***outside*** of what Medicare covers, Fidelity Investments, an organization that has tracked retiree health care costs for more than a decade, estimates a sixty-five-year-old couple retiring this year will need an estimated $275,00 to cover health care costs in retirement. That doesn't include long-term care, and it doesn't reflect what happens to those who retire early (either by choice or by force).[24]

I know of plenty of well-educated, intelligent people who tell me they can't understand Medicare. So, don't feel like the Lone Ranger if it baffles you, too; all the more reason to make sure you work with a specialist who can walk you through all your options. And do this ***before*** you retire, not on the day you retire.

---

[24]Katie Lobosco. CNN Money. Aug. 14, 2017. "Health care will cost couples $275,000 in retirement." http://money.cnn.com/2017/08/24/retirement/health-care-cost-retirement/index.html.

CHAPTER 9

The Affordable Care Act

If you are retiring before the age of sixty-five, you may have to seek out your own coverage from a private insurer. This is something you should look into before retirement. Some employers offer a continuation of coverage until sixty-five, which may be more or less expensive than seeking out your own coverage. If you are seeking out your own coverage, then you will need to tread lightly, as the "Patient Protection and Affordable Care Act of 2010," also known as the Affordable Care Act (or Obamacare) will come into play. While President Donald Trump has been emphatic about repealing that legislation, 2018 passed without a successful effort to repeal or replace it. While Congress notably wrote through the individual mandate in the 2017 tax law, the tax penalty for noncompliance remained in effect through 2018. This means if you were uninsured for very long in January through December that year, you may have to pay a penalty on your 2018 taxes. [25]

While average premium prices have increased for 2019, the subsidies for plans purchased from states or the health care exchanges are still in effect. Here is another area where some good tax planning will be necessary, since your subsidy is based on your *annual*

---

[25] Ryan Kennelly. Health Agents. December 7, 2018. "What is the Penalty for Not Having Health Insurance in 2019?" https://help.ihealthagents.com/hc/en-us/articles/115001888334-What-is-the-penalty-for-not-having-health-insurance-in-2019-.

taxable income. Even if you have a million dollars in investable assets, as long as your *taxable* income does not exceed certain thresholds, you will still receive a subsidy.

According to healthinsurance.org, a resource for self-employed persons seeking to understand their health insurance options, "In 2017, 84 percent of exchange enrollees received premium subsidies that covered an average of two-thirds of the total premiums."[26]

The upper limit for subsidy eligibility for plans purchased during the 2019 open enrollment period can be as high as $100,400 per year for a family of four. Keep in mind, that is *taxable* income. This is where it may make sense to take distributions from both tax-deferred and after-tax investment accounts to satisfy your retirement income needs in order to keep your health insurance costs low. You could actually end up paying more for Medicare than you do for traditional health insurance.

I'm certainly not here to take a political stance, and I'm not here to give you specific advice on what direction you should take for health insurance. It is important that, no matter where your politics lie, you not only recognize the expense, but the huge opportunities for cost savings you may have with some prudent planning.

[26] Louise Norris. HealthInsurance.org. Dec. 7, 2018. "Your guide to buying individual health insurance." https://www.healthinsurance.org/#subsidies. Accessed Dec. 11, 2018.

CHAPTER 10

Risks to Your Income Plan

One of the biggest risks to your retirement income is just simply losing money. As Warren Buffett says about investing:

- Rule No. 1 – Don't lose money.
- Rule No. 2 – Don't forget Rule No.1.

While this quote by the famous investor may seem humorous, it holds real merit. I grew up in a conservative family with a conservative investment philosophy, and it means the world to me. That is why I want to take the time to outline a number of investments that may hold more risks than you are aware of.

Please keep in mind, there is nothing wrong with any of the following investments. They have their place, as long as you understand the risks you are taking. Unfortunately, your advisor may not have informed you of the risks they contain because of bias or lack of education. Also, some advisors may have no other option but to put your retirement income at risk. It could be they are only licensed to sell at-risk investment products. Again, this doesn't make them bad people; they are just selling what they are allowed to sell, whether by choice or because that is all they are allowed to offer because of the company they work for.

The barriers of entry into the financial advice industry are disgustingly low. Someone could be advising you on your life's savings without a high school level of education after passing a simple exam taking a couple of hours to complete. This is why it is so important for you to do your own research on the background and education of the advisor you choose.

Just as you wouldn't permit a stranger without a "Dr." before his name to operate on your heart, you shouldn't let anyone operate on your life's savings without proving they have an acceptable level of certification and experience.

Risky Investments

REITs

Real estate investment trusts. I want to start with REITs because they have been greatly misrepresented over the last several years by brokers and financial advisors. These vehicles are a legitimate investment option for the right investor, but they are definitely not for everyone. In the interests of full disclosure, I personally own REITs, but in very small amounts, and in proportion to my investable assets (less than 10 percent). Why? Because I understand the risks inherit in these investments. These vehicles have been touted for their consistent delivery of dividend income, as well as lack of correlation with the stock market. This does not make them safe by any means.

There are two types of real estate trusts: There are **non-traded** real estate trusts and **traded** real estate trusts. A traded real estate trust trades just like a stock. They tend to pay lower dividends, and the share price bounces up and down every single day in the stock market. In contrast, a non-traded real estate trust does not trade like a stock. In fact, you give up liquidity when you buy a non-traded real estate trust. These non-traded real estate trusts may never pay you back your original investment. Since it is not a publicly traded stock, the market for these investments is very small. Think of non-traded REITs as investing in a private company — a bakery for example. That bakery is hopefully going to pay you some income from year to year. Hopefully, the bakery will expand and grow and the shares you own in that bakery will become more valuable. Then, the bakery may get big enough to begin trading on the New York Stock Exchange, giving you the opportunity to sell the stock. However, if the bakery does not expand, you may never get back your original investment, and your dividend distribution could even cease. The worst-case scenario could be the bakery filing for bankruptcy, and you never getting back your original investment.

The opportunity for big returns in real estate investment trusts, especially non-traded REITs, makes them very attractive. However, I have been outraged at times seeing bankers and financial advisors moving large portions of retirees' life savings into these investments after selling them on the notion that they are taking stock market risk off the table, while at the same time convincing them they will receive a stable and reliable income from them.

Bonds

I often hear people say they are using bonds to follow the "Rule of One Hundred." The Rule of One Hundred is an axiom of investing that states you should take your age, subtract it from One Hundred, and that's the maximum amount of risk you should have in your investment portfolio. While this is just a rule of thumb, it's a good one. Especially if you are going it alone without a real retirement strategy.

However, if you are sixty years old, and have a portfolio of 60 percent bonds and 40 percent stocks, your entire portfolio is at risk. You are not following the Rule of One Hundred.

The risks of corporate bonds, as well as municipal bonds, are often underestimated and misunderstood. The only types of bonds covered by a legal reserve system that could generally be regarded as safe are government issued bonds, such as Treasury bonds or notes. All other bonds will carry with them not only default risk (the risk of bankruptcy), but also interest rate risk. Interest rate risk is the lesser understood of the two, but is a risk facing retirees of today that hasn't been a concern for over thirty years. As interest rates go down, bond prices go up. Note the following interest rate chart:

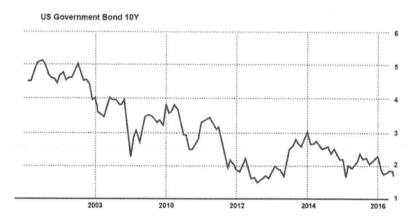

US Government Bond 10Y

Source: www.tradingeconomics.com | U.S. Department of the Treasury

Everything moves in cycles and we are on the cusp of entering the next rising interest rate cycle. Your parents didn't have to endure this, the old stock/bond mix worked out fine for them. But this time it really is different. Now, I don't know when interest rates will rise, or how fast for that matter, but at some point the cycle will begin and you need to be prepared. This is where it pays to begin thinking outside the box, using investment vehicles that can give you a true guarantee of principal with bond-like returns.

Sequence of Returns Risk

Morningstar Inc., a Chicago-based investment research and management firm, has done studies on this feature of saving and investing for retirement that show just how treacherous timing can be to the unsuspecting retirees who are putting their faith solely in the stock market to carry them through their golden years. The trap is called "Sequence of Returns:"

> "The point in time that a person chooses to retire will affect the ability of their portfolio to last throughout retirement," says Morningstar researcher Timothy Strauts.

The general idea is that someone who retires just before or during a dip in the market will have a different experience with their investments and retirement savings than others who retire at different times in the market cycle.

The idea that bad timing can take a bite out of your retirement security is driven home by illustrations that demonstrate how starting withdrawals just as a bear market hits can seriously impair the sustainability of a retirement portfolio over time.

The following charts come from a report from Thornburg Investment Management. The first is the S&P 500 returns from 1989 to 2008 laid next to those exact same returns in reverse. Same numbers, same overall average return.

Figure 1

S&P 500 Index Sequence Of Returns

Year	1989–2008 Sequence	2008–1989 Sequence
1	31.69	–37.00
2	–3.11	5.49
3	30.47	15.84
4	7.62	4.91
5	10.08	10.88
6	1.32	28.68
7	37.58	–22.10
8	22.96	–11.88
9	33.36	–9.11
10	28.58	21.04
11	21.04	28.58
12	–9.11	33.36
13	–11.88	22.96
14	–22.10	37.58
15	28.68	1.32
16	10.88	10.08
17	4.91	7.62
18	15.84	30.47
19	5.49	–3.11
20	–37.00	31.69
Average Annual Return	**8.43%**	**8.43%**

Past performances does not guarantee future results.
Source: S&P 500

The second chart represents two hypothetical portfolios with identical starting amounts ($1 million), both containing 100 percent stock portfolios that mimic the S&P 500. One of the portfolios will experience the market returns of 1989 to 2008, the other will experience the reversed set of returns. Again, same average. You'll notice each portfolio receives the same rates of growth. The only difference is the sequence in which these returns occurred. Keep in mind, this example doesn't include annual withdrawals, which will exacerbate the effects of market downturns in a portfolio.

Figure 2

Sequence Of Returns Impact On A Hypothetical $1 Million Investment Undergoing Systematic Withdrawals *(Using A 100% Equity Portfolio)*

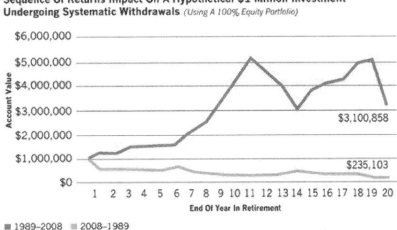

■ 1989–2008 ■ 2008–1989

Hypothetical investment for both sequences consists of 100% equities, represented by the S&P 500 Index.
Past performance does not guarantee future results.
Source: Thornburg Investment Management

So, let's see the result. Portfolio No. 1 increased substantially over time. It TRIPLED in value. Yet, it's counterpart—which experience the exact same returns, just in reverse order—has suffered a great loss. You can rerun this scenario in any market period; a comparison of someone who retired in the early nineties to someone retiring in the throes of the Great Recession might look similar.

So, what's the point? That timing matters—a portfolio that is hit early on in retirement simultaneously by both a bear market and withdrawals will not be able to sustain wealth...even if you experience good returns in later years.[27]

You can't influence when you are born, therefore you can't influence when you will reach retirement age. But you can manage

---

[27] Timothy Strauts. Morningstar. July 7, 2015. "How Bad Timing Can Bite in Retirement." http://www.morningstar.com/cover/videocenter.aspx?id=705503. Accessed Aug. 15, 2016.

your risk through planning and strategy. The first ten years of your retirement, both before and after your retirement date, will be the most vital to the success of your retirement income strategy. That is why I like to call this the Retirement Red Zone. Investment losses during this time frame can make or break a retirement income strategy. This is why it is so important to not only plan well ahead of retirement, but begin greatly reducing market risk at this point in your life.

Reverse Dollar-Cost Averaging

When you are a young investor in your accumulation years, dollar-cost averaging is a valuable investment technique that takes advantage of the volatility of the stock market to reduce cost over time. If you have had a 401(k), 403(b), 457, or some other qualified retirement plan with your employer, you probably contributed to it at regular intervals over your working years. When the market dipped, and share prices fell, no problem — your contribution bought more shares. When the market rose and share prices rose, no problem — your account got fatter. Over time, this process reduced your overall cost of buying into the stock market.

Once you enter retirement, however, the process is usually reversed. Now, instead of making regular contributions you are making regular withdrawals. You withdraw the same amount when share prices fall, and the same amount when share prices rise. It is very easy to violate the old axiom of "sell high and buy low," because our income needs are fixed. So the DCA that helped us in our accumulation years comes back to bite us in our retirement years *if we do not plan carefully.*

The "4 Percent Withdrawal" Myth

Brokerage firms and some financial advisors who are tethered solely to the stock market have promoted what they call the "4 percent withdrawal rule" of investing as a sure-fire way to retire without running out of money. According to their math, if you have $1 million in a brokerage account, the 4 percent withdrawal rule says that you should be able to withdraw 4 percent from the account annually ($40,000), and even add slightly to that figure each year for inflation, and never run out of money in retirement. The concept hinges on rebalancing the account each year, achieving just the right mixture of stocks and bonds. The concept may have been valid in the 1990s when the stock market was on a steady upswing, but it simply doesn't work anymore in the economy of the twenty-first century.

The 4 percent theory was the brainchild of three professors at Trinity University in San Antonio, Texas, in the mid-1990s and made popular in an article by William Bengen, "Determining Withdrawal Rates Using Historical Data," first published in October 1994 in Journal of Financial Planning-Denver. All of their calculations and projections were based on stock market data available at the time. When the 1990s ended with the bursting of the tech bubble in 2000, and a sideways market dominated the market for the next decade, the 4 percent withdrawal rule lost its validity. The problem is, there are still some die-hard advisors who still promote it because it suits their aims to sell stock, and too many investors who are still drinking the Kool-Aid.

Other factors that make the 4 percent rule invalid include the fact that most Americans are not super wealthy, and people are living longer in retirement these days, not to mention a near-zero interest-rate environment, resulting in dramatic underperformance of the bond portion of your portfolio.

Protecting Against Inflation

Inflation is one of those risks you will face in retirement that is often misunderstood and too often overstated. Yes, you should prepare for it, but don't over-prepare. If you look at the history of consumer prices in America, you will see just how erratic inflation has been.

My finance professor often said that inflation has been through "its go-go years, its slow-go years, and its no-go years."

No one who lived through the 1970s and early 1980s will forget seeing interest rates go from 6 percent to 18 percent and prices on everything from butter to

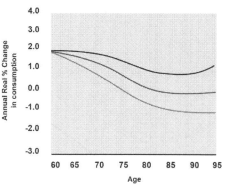

Retirement Income Targets

Annual Real Change in Consumption

Lifetime Real Income Target, Age 65 Retiree

gasoline double and triple. Retirees on fixed incomes were shell-shocked when they approached the checkout counter at their local supermarket. The grocery cart they were accustomed to paying $40 for now cost them $140!

But those years of inflation were an anomaly, a big economic glitch, according to Wharton School Professor of Finance Jeremy Sigel, who, in his book, "Stocks for the Long Run: A Guide for Long Term Growth," called stocks "the greatest failure of American macroeconomic policy in the postwar period." [28]

Could it happen again? Perhaps, but history and common sense would indicate otherwise. My finance professor in college often stated that retirees will go through their "go-go years, slow-go years, and no-go years." In other words, they'll spend less throughout their retirement years as their lifestyle changes. However, this is rarely, if ever, factored into an income strategy put together by a financial planner and the results are often extremely discouraging for pre-retirees resulting in often extremely over-exaggerated asset and income needs.

---

[28] Jeremy Sigel. 1994. "Stocks for the Long Run."

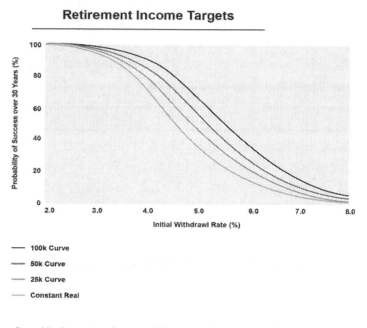

Source: https://corporate.morningstar.com/ib/documents/methodologydocuments/researchpapers/blanchett_true-cost-of-retirement.pdf

David Blanchett, head of Retirement Research at Morningstar Investment Management, produced a study entitled "Estimating the True Cost of Retirement" that points out that, while general inflation can be expected to average around 3 percent in the foreseeable future, spending by retirees will also decline as they age.[29] Retirees will spend more in their early years, of course, because they are more active. Then, they will steadily decrease their spending as they become less active. This should serve to offset inflation fears somewhat. The most uncertainty comes in the areas of health care and housing.

---

[29] David Blanchett. Morningstar. November 5, 2013. "Estimating the True Cost of Retirement." https://corporate.morningstar.com/ib/documents/methodologydocuments/researchpapers/blanchett_true-cost-of-retirement.pdf.

The Blanchett study also indicates that traditional research over-estimates the amount of money people need to have saved up before they retire.

The bottom line: Don't underestimate or overestimate inflation risk. Take comfort in the fact that it may not be as big a risk as initially stated, but it doesn't mean we shouldn't have a plan to combat it if we encounter it. Just don't let your broker scare you into thinking you need to have all of your investments at risk to combat something as unpredictable as inflation.

CHAPTER 11

Get a Retirement Income Plan

Establishing your retirement income plan may be the most important topic touched on in this book. Every person concerned about their retirement income is either in retirement or planning for retirement — and you need a real plan, not just a bunch of mutual funds that you hope take care of the issue.

You need a strategy that plans for the best but prepares for the worst. I'm going to give you the components of a retirement income plan and talk about why this is so important.

Whether you have a lot saved for retirement or a little, you probably get caught up in the here and now from time to time. You may look at interest rates down at the bank, bonds, annuities, or rates of return in the stock market, then you turn on the news only to see the market is down or up, and all of that thinking is very short-term. A true purpose-based retirement income strategy will give you confidence, or at least the truth, about where you stand in retirement. This is why I truly believe all retirees should have their very own, personalized, purpose-based retirement income strategy, regardless of where they stand today.

A "***purpose-based***" retirement income strategy is simply a snapshot of where you stand today, an isolation of the different risks you will face, and a picture of the future under different assumptions. This is what will give you the ability to sleep well during your retirement years.

Let's talk about some of the basic steps necessary in developing a good retirement income plan. Here are the steps:

Emergency fund: Factor in contingencies and create a side fund, to meet the big contingencies. These might be things like additional health care costs not covered by Medicare, or big emergencies, such as helping the kids or home maintenance costs. We are creating a side fund here so that you have several groups of money. One for emergencies, a side fund, a fund with liquidity for all the other things, the next for the production of consistent and reliable retirement income for as long as you live. Typically, we would recommend somewhere between six and twelve months of your monthly expenses be set aside and not counted into the retirement equation.

Income and expense: Next, we need to determine your expenses. This will require that you do a good job of tracking and watching your budget. So pretend you are retired today (and maybe you already are). How much do you want coming into the household every single month in cash? Think of this as a net number, after taxes. This is CRUCIAL, this is the number that will be used to structure your entire purpose-based retirement strategy. Don't overcomplicate this, and don't think about inflation, or rate of return on investments. Just write down the money you want coming into the house every single month net after taxes. Let's say your number is $5,000. Write that number down.

Inflation: The next thing we want to do is factor inflation into the mix. For now, let's just keep this really simple. Let's set aside enough to increase your monthly income by 20 percent at any time, with a 4 percent withdrawal from this bucket. So, for a $60,000 annual income that would be $12,000 divided by 4 percent. That gives us $300,000. So even though historically we shouldn't need to touch these funds, we have a backup plan. Of course, we will have to factor in any estimated inflation adjustments you may have from other sources of income, such as your pension or Social Security. I just want to give you a picture of the process here.

Estate: Now that we have set aside funds for emergencies, income needs, and inflation protection, what other reason might you need to draw off of your remaining life savings? Your answer should be health care. And not just any type of health care, but long-term care or home health care, assisted living, or nursing home care. This is something we may want to explore buying insurance to cover.

There are different types of long-term care insurance. There's the old-fashioned kind, where you pay a premium for the rest of your life, and may never get anything back if you never use it. Then there's the new kind, that's kind of a hybrid, where, if you never use the long-term care, you still get all your money back, or your beneficiaries may get it back. In either case, you should be exploring your options for covering that risk.

Once we have satisfied your emergency needs, income needs, inflation needs, and health care needs, we can then explore ways to maximize what I like to refer to as your "never" money, and the best way to maximize your legacy. This will also include your basic estate planning documents at a bare minimum. The complexity of your legal planning will be dependent on the size of your estate and will require some form of legal counsel — don't forget this step or you could leave a mess for your beneficiaries and loved ones.

CHAPTER 12

Pension Buyouts: Do Some Calculations Before You Decide

I f you are one of the lucky few retirees who have a pension to take you through your retirement years, then this section is for you.

The letter no doubt arrived unexpectedly. A company you once worked for has an extraordinary proposal for you. You are due a monthly pension when you hit retirement age, but the company is offering to pay you a hefty lump sum right now to buy out your pension.

Do nothing and your pension situation continues as is. Accept the buyout and you'll have a large chunk of money to invest toward retirement. But you can no longer expect to get that monthly check the company had promised when you retire. Suddenly, you have a major financial decision to make that could have a significant impact on your retirement.

Initially, you may even be puzzled about why that company you once worked for is so interested in buying out your pension. Low interest rates represent one reason. Many of these pensions had anticipated that interest rates would be higher and that the money in the pension fund would be growing at a faster pace. These pension funds invest in equities and bonds just like you might find in your

401(k)s and IRAs. According to James Comtois at Pensions & Investments, "The aggregate funded status of the 100 largest U.S. public pension plans dipped slightly to an estimated 71.2 percent as of June 30 [2018], down from 71.4 percent as of March 31."[30] With projected rates of return of over 7 percent in order to succeed, you might be able to see how this is becoming a problem. People are living longer, too. That's great for you, but it means extra years of monthly payments that the pension folks hadn't counted on. That combination has led most companies to try to get out of the pension game as quickly as possible. If every pensioner stays in the plan, they are in trouble. They need to cut some costs and some liability.

So what should you do when that lump-sum offer arrives?

First, sit down with a trusted advisor who can provide you some education and consultation, because there's no one-size-fits-all solution here. Both the specific terms of the buyout and your individual situation play a role in whether you should accept the lump sum, or hold steady and wait for that monthly pension check down the road. One of the most important things an advisor can do for you is providing you with the facts, so you can make your own decision. Advisors who just tell you what you need to do aren't doing their job. They should empower you to make your own decision. Otherwise, whose interests are they looking out for?

For example, suppose your pension is set at $2,000 a month. That might not sound like much, but it comes to $24,000 a year. Over twenty-five years of retirement, that's close to $600,000. If you were going to take an annual withdrawal from your retirement savings, you would need close to $400,000 at a 4 percent annual return in order to match the pension over twenty-five years. That's the kind of information you should take into consideration as you

---

[30] James Comtois. Pensions & Investments. August 6, 2018. "U.S. Public Pension Plans See Funded Status Dip in Second Quarter. – Milliman." https://www.pionline.com/article/20180806/ONLINE/180809900/us-public-pension-plans-see-funded-status-dip-in-second-quarter-8211-milliman.

weigh your decision. Is the lump sum large enough, or can it grow enough, to provide you a similar annual return as those monthly pension payments would give you?

If it would take an 8 to 10 percent rate of return on the lump sum to give you a cash flow equal to the pension payments at your life expectancy, then you'll likely want to stick with the pension. On the other hand, if a low rate of return could provide that same cash flow, you might want to go with the lump sum.

Life Expectancy

Something else to factor into the decision is life expectancy. You can outlive a lump sum, but you can't outlive a pension. At the same time, you can't bequeath that pension payment to your children, but you could leave them the money in the lump sum. Some situations are no-brainers. Let say you are in poor health, and do not expect to live much longer, and there is no spouse in the picture to whom the pension could be transferred. Then it would obviously be a wise course to take the lump sum. Or it could be that you are well-fixed financially from other income sources and simply do not need the pension income. Then your financial goals may be better served to accept a cash buyout of your pension. A third scenario may be that you could use the money from the cash buyout to establish a better income stream from the private market, perhaps with even better benefits than the one offered by the company.

For many people, the answer might be to take the lump sum and put it in an annuity with a guaranteed lifetime withdrawal benefit. That way, they can have a steady income stream that could actually offer a greater income than the pension, along with more flexibility and control over their money.

Oddly enough, I've heard people say they hate annuities, and yet a pension essentially is an annuity. Yet I've never heard anyone say,

"I hate my pension." Guaranteed income comes at a price, but you can't put a price on peace of mind.

Another thing to keep in mind is the backing of the payments. While your pension is backed by the Pension Benefit Guaranty Corporation up to certain limits, your annuity is backed by the strength of the issuing company.

Regardless, when you're offered a lump sum, it's your responsibility to educate yourself about your options and evaluate your goals carefully. Here are some good questions to ask yourself before making your decision:

- Do I have an emergency fund in case of the unexpected?
- How much income will I need to protect my spouse in case of death?
- Do I even need any more income from my investments?
- Do I need that income now or later?
- Are there concerns over the strength of my pension?
- Do I care what is left behind for my children or charity?
- And the most difficult of questions . . . How long will I live?

Whether or not to take your pension as a lump sum may be one of the biggest retirement decisions you will ever make — and it's permanent! If you take the lump sum option, you will be responsible for your own investments and you lose the guarantees associated with your pension.

The survivorship options inside your pension plan are essentially forms of life insurance. You may be able to get more income and leave more assets behind for your family by taking the larger single-life pension and using the difference to purchase life insurance on the private market. That strategy could be less costly and offer more in the way of benefits than you could achieve through your employer.

Pension Maximization Options

The two main options you will have when it comes to your pension are (a) a single life annuity and (b) a joint and survivor annuity. Think of it as life insurance through an annuity provider. Here, you have to ask yourself, am I getting a good deal on life insurance? Or can I do better on the private market?

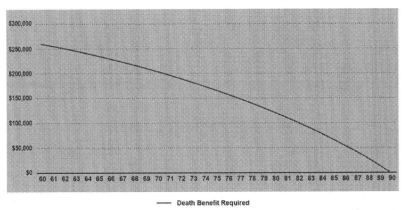

Death Benefit Required for Pension Replacement

⎯ Death Benefit Required

In the accompanying chart, we see an example of pension maximization using private insurance to replace a portion of a pension payout. At age sixty, a worker with a life expectancy of ninety opts to take the higher single life payout, and use insurance from the private sector to guarantee a lump sum for a spouse. In this case, it is a good decision (note the annual savings column).

Let's walk through the example.

Dan and Theresa were able to maintain the same net income as they would have received with the joint and survivor pension option, as well as protection for Theresa in the event of Dan's untimely death. BUT they were also able to provide for two secondary goals. If they BOTH passed away, they would leave the remaining value of the pension behind for their children. And they would also enable the use of a portion of the death benefit to cover the cost of potential long-term health care. This would be accomplished through a policy option called "acceleration of death benefits." Not to mention that, unlike the original pension, they were not required to make a permanent decision. If something were to happen to Theresa, or if their goals merely changed, they could always cancel their life insurance policies, increasing their net income.

This option may not work for everyone. Life insurance is issued contingent on insurability, so health is a consideration. Your unique pension factors also enter into the equation. But it is up to you to understand all of your options at retirement so you can make the best decision for yourself moving forward.

Pension Optimization

The bottom line is this: You may be better off taking the lump sum pension option instead of leaving your pension with your employer. You may be able to achieve a better guaranteed income, greater flexibility, and better benefits on the private annuity market.

Why are pension buyouts becoming a popular option these days? Because many existing pension plans were projected and funded during times of high interest rates, shorter life spans, and during periods of better stock market growth. As a result, many companies offering pensions have realized they may be unable to meet their pension obligations. They have begun offering cash lump sum settlements instead of the lifetime annuities.

If you are making a decision on a pension buyout, choose carefully with your PURPOSE in mind. For example, why would you take a guaranteed lifetime income pension if you don't need the income? Or if you don't have an emergency fund? Maybe you only need a portion of the guaranteed income, and you could use the remaining funds for health care or legacy protection. This is where it pays to evaluate your options on the private annuity market. Your pension is essentially an annuity. So you have to ask yourself, is my pension the best annuity I can get? You may be able to get an annuity in the private market that will offer a better guaranteed income, with the flexibility to make changes in the future, and leave assets behind to your heirs.

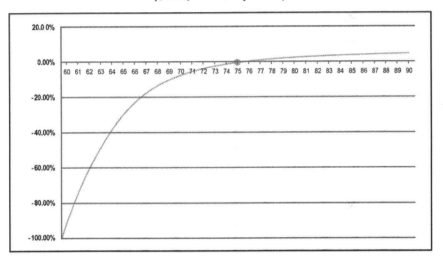

The preceding example illustrates how the internal rate of return can be calculated to determine the break-even point.

CHAPTER 13

Don't Overlook the Odds and Ends of Your 401(k)

efore we climb into this chapter, let me remind readers that this guide is meant to be used as material furthering the educational process regarding things I often discuss with clients during our sessions. While interesting, some of the strategies and concepts might not apply to your individual situation. If you don't own employer stock inside your 401(k), it won't apply to you directly, but it is information you could use to help others. For example, I have one client who worked for a well-known local defense contractor. That contractor's employees own a lot of employer stock. Armed with some of the following information, he was able to pass along to others the strategies that enabled him to save thousands of dollars on taxes, and make some good friends along the way of course.

This is a small section, but a very crucial one if you own employer stock inside your 401(k). This simply cannot be overlooked. I have seen some retirees spend tens of thousands of dollars in unnecessary taxes because they didn't work with a competent financial advisor with a good understanding of tax laws.

If you own employer stock inside of your 401(k), you can take advantage of a little-known tax rule known as Net Unrealized Appreciation. It works like this: When you retire, you have the ability to roll your 401(k) and employer stock over to an IRA. If you do so, when you ultimately take distributions from that IRA, you will be taxed at your highest marginal tax bracket, which could be as much as 37 percent in 2019.[31] With your employer stock, you have another option. Instead of rolling that employer stock over to an IRA you can take it in kind to a taxable brokerage account.

"But Casey," you might be saying, "You just said if I take a distribution from my tax-deferred accounts, I have to pay taxes on the whole distribution!" I see you are paying attention. But there is a little-known provision available for employer stock that allows you to only pay tax on your **cost basis** and **defer taxation** on the appreciation of the stock. If you then sell the stock down the road, the appreciation will be taxed at long-term capital gains rates, which as explained earlier could be taxed as low as 0 percent, and as high as 23.8 percent, including Medicare tax. If you decide to hold onto that stock and pass it on to your heirs, those heirs will receive a step-up in basis to the date of death value, and they could sell the stock without paying any taxes on the appreciation.

Retiring Early? Don't Roll Over Everything!

For those lucky few of you who may be in a position to retire early, this little tip is for you. One of the biggest concerns retirees have when they want to retire early is how to avoid early distribution penalties from their tax-deferred retirement accounts.

This is another area where I have seen greedy or uneducated financial planners cause their clients a ton of pain in the form of unnecessary tax penalties. Several years ago a client came to me. He was age fifty-eight and had retired two years previously, at age fifty-six. When he retired, he found a financial planner with whom he

---

[31] Bankrate. November 28, 2018. "2018-2019 Tax Brackets." https://www.bankrate.com/finance/taxes/tax-brackets.aspx

wanted to work. The advisor had him roll over his entire 401(k) into an IRA, telling the client that, unfortunately, he would have to begin paying taxes on the income he withdrew from the IRA. Not only that, but he would also be subject to a 10 percent penalty on those distributions, because he was under the age of fifty-nine-and-one-half. So, for over two years the man withdrew around $100,000 from his retirement account, and forked over not only the taxes, but approximately $20,000 in tax penalties.

All of this could have been avoided, had he simply left his re-quired pre-fifty-nine-and-one-half income inside of his 401(k). You see, a 401(k) operates under different rules than an IRA. If you separate from service after the age of fifty-five, you can take distri-butions from your 401(k) without paying tax penalties as you would with an IRA. Now, this doesn't mean you should leave everything in your 401(k) if you plan to retire. You can often get lower cost, more flexibility, and better options outside of your 401(k). But it may make sense to leave *some* of your 401(k) *inside* that account if you are retiring before the age of fifty-nine-and-one-half.

CHAPTER 14

Reducing Hidden Fees and Unnecessary Expenses

W hen Benjamin Franklin said "a penny saved is a penny earned," he wasn't just whistling Dixie. Every dollar you pay in investment expenses and hidden fees within the financial instruments you are using to fund your eventual retirement is a dollar that cannot earn interest and cannot support your lifestyle. Investment fees and expenses that lurk behind the closed doors in your investment accounts compose one of the most significant impediments to retirement success today.

Perhaps no one in the investment community has done more to bring to light the negative effect of hidden fees in mutual funds than John C. "Jack" Bogel, founder and retired CEO of the Vanguard Group. In his article, "The Arithmetic of 'All-In' Investment Expenses," Bogel makes it clear that, in mutual fund investing, what we see is not always what we get.

> "For years and years — decades really — the standard in comparing costs in mutual funds has been to take their total expense ratio in the mutual fund annual report, which is usually between 1-2 percent. There are a lot of costs that aren't in the expense ratio — transaction costs in the portfolio activity, cash drags, taxes, and

investment behavior costs, such as picking the wrong funds at the wrong time." [32]

If you are like most investors, you are probably completely unaware of these hidden costs. I have met with hundreds of investors over the years, and have yet to find one of them who knows the full extent to which these fees impede their financial growth. These fees are like barnacles on the bottom of a boat. They slow you down, and they hide below the waterline, and invisible until someone points them out.

There are some things that are beyond our control. What will the stock market do tomorrow, two weeks from now, next year, or the next ten years? I don't know. Neither do you. Anyone who tells you they know is lying. I have to smile sometimes when a prospective client asks, "How much more of a return can you get me from my market investments than my current advisor?" The closest thing I have to a crystal ball is one of those snow globes that someone gave me as a souvenir from their trip to Japan, and it isn't talking!

But here's something you can control, much like your taxes, that will absolutely increase your returns and put more of your money in your pocket — *reducing your fees and expenses!*

Mutual Funds

There are two types of mutual fund expenses that work against an investor's goals: **stated** and **unstated** expenses. Together, they create a formidable hurdle for your retirement income.

You are most likely familiar with the stated expenses that we will find inside of a typical mutual fund. They are in the prospectus —

[32] John C. Bogle. Financial Analysts Journal. January/February 2014. "The Arithmetic of "All In" Investment Expenses." http://johncbogle.com/wordpress/wp-content/uploads/2010/04/FAJ-All-In-Investment-Expenses-Jan-Feb-2014.pdf.

that one-hundred-page, plastic-wrapped, phone-book-sized document that you receive in the mail once per year. It's written in a hard-to-see four-point type font, so you probably set it to one side, knowing you should take a day out of your schedule and read it, but you just never get around to it. So, eventually it lands in the circle file (waste basket) along with the day's junk mail. And that is where the **stated** expenses are found. There you will encounter a number called the "average expense ratio." This represents costs such as administrative fees, management fees, marketing fees, and loads.

According to the Investment Company Institute, the average expense ratio in an equity mutual fund is 1.4 percent per year. Keep in mind, this is just an average. Your expenses could be lower or significantly higher than this. I have personally seen expense ratios exceeding 3 percent annually, especially in smaller funds where there are fewer investors available to spread out these costs.

While you may be with "stated" expenses, you may be less familiar with, or completely unaware of, the "unstated" expenses associated with mutual funds. One reason for this is they are more difficult to quantify, and companies aren't required to disclose them by law — not yet, anyway. I hope this changes in the near future.

I think it is your right to know *exactly* what you are paying for any type of service, whether that be investment-related or otherwise. These expenses, much like an iceberg, can dwarf the stated costs as is easily seen in the preceding illustration.

These expenses include trading costs, trading commissions, market impact costs, and even taxes (as we discussed earlier). The largest of these undisclosed expenses are the trading costs.

Trading Costs

Trading costs are found in all securities transactions, but can be greatly magnified in large, very actively managed funds. Every time a mutual fund manager buys or sells a security, the fund incurs a small trading cost. The more actively traded a mutual fund is, the higher the trading costs are for the fund, and its shareholders. A 2009 study of thousands of U.S. equity mutual funds discovered trading costs investors, on average, 1.44 percent per year. Stephen Horan, of the CFA institute (a nonprofit professional organization), estimates these costs to be 1-3 percent annually for equity funds. These trading costs are on top of the expense ratio previously disclosed.[33] So if we do some simple math, we can see how quickly the cost of your mutual fund alone can get over 3 percent annually. On a $500,000 portfolio, that's equivalent to $15,000 per year — *and we haven't even gotten to advisor fees yet!*

Advisory Fees

You may pay your advisor in the form of an annual management fee for investment selection. These advisory fees can range anywhere from 1-2 percent annually. Now, think about what your expenses are if your advisor is charging you an annual advisory fee, then turning around and investing those hard-earned dollars into

---

[33] Stephen Horan. CFA Institute. May 3, 2011. "The New Wealth Management."

equity based mutual funds. With a 1 percent advisory fee, you can do some simple math to see how your expenses could quickly rise closer to 4 percent annually. On a $500,000 portfolio, that's $20,000 per year! Gone! Money that you could have used for your retirement income instead.

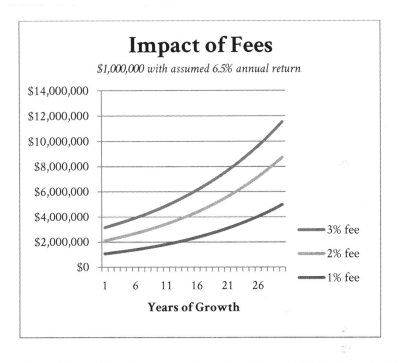

Financial straight-shooter and author John Pollock wrote in his book, "The Nest Egg Cookbook":

> "If you are paying an advisor 1 percent or so for his fee, and the advisor is then turning around and putting you in mutual funds with annual expense ratios of around 1.5 percent, your total investing costs are way too high. A financial advisor who charges a flat management fee should be focused on individual stocks or

very low-cost funds, such as index funds, market funds or ETFs."[34]

Amen to that!

Variable Annuities

When you peel back its layers, variable annuities are essentially stock market investments in an annuity wrapper. Your money is invested in what amounts to mutual funds, only tax deferred. Mutual funds can lose money. There are fees associated with these investments. I am not saying that variable annuities are not suitable investments for some folks. They couldn't exist if they weren't. But you need to go into them with your eyes wide open.

There are some guarantees associated with variable annuities, true, but they also have risks and expenses that fixed annuities don't have.

Here's what Fidelity says about variable annuities under the heading, "A Shopper's Guide to Annuity Fees:"[35]

> "deferred variable annuities can include insurance charges, investment management fees, surrender charges, and rider charges, yet they tend to have a significant degree of variability . . . These features may include both death benefits and living benefits, which come at an additional cost. If these are of interest to you, take some time to research how each feature works (e.g., whether it applies when you are alive or if you die) and consider its price tag. Then, evaluate whether that rider works for your specific situation when considering a variable annuity. It's also important to review the prospectus thoroughly.

---

[34] John Pollock. March 10, 2010. "The Nest Egg Cookbook."

[35] Fidelity Viewpoints. Fidelity. April 9, 2018. "A Shopper's Guide to Annuity Fees." https://www.fidelity.com/viewpoints/retirement/shoppers-guide-to-annuity-fees

Basically, evaluate anything before investing in it. Period.

Surrender Charges

Variable annuities, like fixed annuities, have surrender charges for early withdrawal. Nothing wrong with that, it's just that if an investor doesn't understand that going in, they could get blindsided.

Mortality and Expense Risk Charges

Here is where fixed and variable annuities vary greatly. VAs have mortality and expense risk charges, whereas no such fees exist in fixed annuities. What are these "mortality and expense risk charges?" The SEC describes them this way:[36]

> "This charge is equal to a certain percentage of your account value, typically in the range of 1.25 percent per year. This charge compensates the insurance company for insurance risks it assumes under the annuity contract. Profit from the mortality and expense risk charge is sometimes used to pay the insurer's costs of selling the variable annuity, such as a commission paid to your financial professional for selling the variable annuity to you."

Administrative Fees

These are fees you pay for record-keeping and other administrative expenses. This may be charged as a flat account maintenance fee (perhaps $25 or $30 per year) or as a percentage of your account value (typically in the range of 0.15 percent per year).

Underlying Fund Expenses

This is a big one. "Underlying fund expenses" translates to your paying the cost of buying and selling securities. In other words, every time a trade is made in the stock market on behalf of your

---

[36] Securities and Exchange Commission. "Variable Annuities: What You Should Know." https://www.sec.gov/investor/pubs/varannty.htm.

variable annuity account, you are paying for that trade. Where does that money come from? The value of the sub-accounts within your variable annuity contract. Underlying fund expenses should simply be the expense ratio in addition to internal unstated costs of the fund, which would include trading costs. These costs were explained earlier in the mutual fund description, as the underlying investments are always mutual funds.

I have said it before, but it bears repeating: Every dollar you pay in fees, loads, and commissions is a dollar that cannot be working for you.

Fees and Charges for Insurance Features

Please remember that a variable annuity is both a security product and an insurance product. One of the biggest reasons stockbrokers like to sell variable annuities to their clients is because they can offer them certain features that an outright market investment would not contain. A variable annuity contract, for example, may contain an option such as a stepped-up death benefit, long-term care insurance, and a provision where, if the account loses money, a tacked-on insurance policy would pay the variable annuity owner's heirs the full amount invested. But here's what you need to know. All of those bells and whistles come with additional fees and charges leading to MASSIVE retirement inefficiency. Make sure you read the prospectus carefully and know what you are paying for each of these and ask your insurance professional to help you determine if the coverage is worth the premium.

One point of confusion with variable annuities is the death benefit. The variable annuity owner may have a rude awakening if the investment portion of his account loses a significant amount of the original principal. The guarantees provided by the insurance company will not benefit the owner of the contract, only his heirs. Was the fee associated with that insurance guarantee bundled inside the variable annuity wrapper competitive with the premium on an ordinary life insurance policy? It most definitely wasn't tax free, as you would find with life insurance. So, was this really the most efficient way to preserve your legacy?

People love the sound of the word "guarantee" with any investment. But if you received any sort of so-called "guarantee," it probably came in the form of an income or death benefit guarantee. You can bet you had to pay for that. These sometimes come at a cost of more than 2 percent per year.

CHAPTER 15

Choose the Right Financial Planner

I want to offer you a few important points you should keep in mind when you're trying to find the right financial advisor for you and your family. I'm not always the right fit for the people who come into our office, and they aren't always the right fit for us. This has to be a mutual decision on behalf of both parties, as you could be starting a lifelong relationship. That is, if your advisor isn't near retirement age for themselves, but that's an entirely different story.

Independence

It is incredibly important to find a financial advisor who is independent, not an employee of a large firm. There are many firms at which brokers and advisors can work. I started in the business as an employee of a large brokerage firm, and we employees were told what products and funds to recommend. We were told that what we had to sell was perfect for everyone.

I soon came to realize this was the wrong approach, but unfortunately, this still goes on today. During those days, I would often be using a tool that I was told to sell, and would soon find that a tool my dad could use as an independent financial advisor was lower in cost with more benefits!

Let's take, for example, a large Wall Street brokerage firm. First of all, if you work for such a firm, the people you work with are employees of that firm, so their primary responsibility is to that firm, not to you as the client. Their job is to increase shareholder value for that particular firm. You're just a customer. However, if you work with an independent financial advisor, then you are the only person to whom that advisor answers. An ethical independent advisor does not have an agenda or a list of stocks to push. This is why it is so vital that you work with an independent advisor who can always use the best tool for the job and answer only to you.

Chemistry

The second important consideration is "chemistry." It's very important that you feel the person you are talking to understands you. If you are a husband and wife, make sure the person talks to both of you. Make sure the advisor also listens to both of you. If for one moment you feel that a broker is dismissing you or your feelings, or is insulting, or comes across as arrogant, this is the wrong person to work with. You need to choose an advisor who understands you, who listens to you, and who will put together a financial plan that fits your needs and goals.

Empathy

Does the advisor understand you and feel like you do when it comes to your important issues? You may have a special-needs child who requires special planning. You may come from a very poor family, one that lived through the Great Depression, and you're worried about running out of money. Can that advisor relate? It's critical that the advisor listen and feel empathy for your particular fears. Another clue that you're working with the wrong advisor is if he or she does not understand or does not listen.

Community Recognition

The broker or advisor you choose should have a recognized name in the community. Let's think about a company like Google. In Palo Alto, if somebody even writes the word "Google" on a sign, Google comes after them to take that word down. Why? Google makes sure that it has the legal right to force the issue. Why? They will do it simply because it wants to protect their reputation, which they feel is second to none. Other companies that have a very high level of brand recognition such as McDonald's and Pepsi will do almost anything to protect that brand.

Conscientious firms may decide not to take certain customers, because they worry that those customers might be the complaining type, and the companies want to protect their reputation and their brand. The same goes for financial advisors. Financial advisors who have a recognized name in a community will be very careful to bend over backward to do the right thing. Why? Because they have spent years building their strong reputations, and they don't want anything to tarnish them. Choose an advisor who has a well-recognized name in the community.

Education

Not much is required to hang out one's shingle as a financial advisor. The unfortunate truth is the majority of financial advisors lack the education, knowledge, credentials, and experience that are required to carry you through the ups and downs of your golden years. The bar for entry into the financial profession has been set quite low. Many firms do not even require a college degree. Many states, in fact, require no formal education or certification at all in order to set up shop as a financial advisor. In contrast, however, some advisors put themselves through grueling, rigorous and extensive educational programs to obtain such designations as CERTIFIED FINANCIAL PLANNER™ professional, and Chartered Financial Analyst (CFA®). So, asking for an advisor's education and experience is fundamental in your search. I believe it should be one of the first questions you ask.

In addition, there are literally hundreds of designations and certifications that are deceptively impressive. Many advisors hold impressive-sounding credentials, some of which represent impressive achievements, but most do not. Before selecting your advisor, make sure that you understand what his or her credentials really represent. For instance, a CERTIFIED FINANCIAL PLANNER™ professional now must have:

- Graduated with a bachelor's degree (or higher) from an accredited college or university
- Taken and passed eighteen to twenty-four hours of certificate-level coursework encompassing the areas of financial planning, insurance planning, investment planning, income tax planning, retirement planning, estate planning, and interpersonal communication
- Completed the CFP Board's Financial Plan Development Course, requiring presentation of a financial plan to the CFP Board
- Completed a pass/fail ten-hour exam over one-and-one-half days at a secure facility
- Took three years of full-time relevant personal financial planning experience, or two years of apprenticeship experience that meets additional requirements
- Passed the CFP Board's Fitness Standards for Candidates and Registrants
- Completed thirty hours of continuing education every two years

In sharp contrast, the Certified Retirement Financial Advisor Certification Board only requires a four-day classroom course, no prior work experience, and no higher education. And although you're required to complete fifteen hours of continuing education per year, everything can be taken online by simply bypassing the class and taking a quiz. While this designation may sound very similar to a CERTIFIED FINANCIAL PLANNER™, the two are in no way comparable. The financial services industry requires financial advisors to establish credibility with their clients. For this reason, an entire credentialing industry now exists to satisfy industry demand. Believe it or not, you could "earn" all of these credentials in less than thirty days — no prior work experience required!

- CAC — Certified Annuity Consultant — one-day class
- APP — Asset Protection Planner — twelve-hour online or in-person
- LTCIS — Long-Term Care Insurance Strategist — two-day class
- AIF — Accredited Investment Fiduciary — two-and-one-half-day class
- CCPS — Certified College Planning Specialist — eighteen to twenty-five hours self-study
- CWPP — Certified Wealth Preservation Planner — twenty-four hours online or in person
- CFG — Certified Financial Gerontologist — twenty-four hours self-study
- CSC — Certified Senior Consultant — twenty-five hours self-study
- CSA — Certified Senior Advisor — three-and-one-half-day "live" class
- AIFA — Accredited Investment Fiduciary Auditor — three-and-one-half-day class
- CDS — Certified Divorce Specialist — four-day workshop

- CRFA — Certified Retirement Financial Advisor — four-day class

Experience

The failure rate for legitimate financial advisors is incredibly high. It is one of the most difficult professions to succeed in, with the long hours and the high level of education required. According to Andre Cappon, president of the CBM Group, only 15 percent of advisors in training make it through their fourth year. That is why I recommend you find an advisor with a minimum of five years in practice. Many financial advisors have a high level of sales experience and are extremely charismatic, but personality can only take you so far.

Your Investment Team

When looking for your retirement advisor, recognize the value of a team approach. In retirement, your financial life becomes much more complicated. You will need to ensure that all of your bases are covered, mainly those of taxation, estate planning, and financial planning. Your retirement advisor should act as the quarterback of this team, assisting you with not only developing and implementing your plan, but bringing a team of experts to the table.

In the world of finance, we all have our areas of expertise. The Certified Public Accountant (CPA) has extensive experience in the area of accounting and tax. The attorney who specializes in estate planning will naturally have extensive experience in estate law. Your financial professional should have general knowledge and experience in both of these areas as well as in the area of handling your investments, even though he or she specializes in the latter. You will most likely need all of these experts to work as a team, with your financial advisor acting as quarterback or general contractor.

Commonsense Investing

Finally, a word about commonsense investing.

They make vehicles these days that will operate on both land and water. You can drive right from land right into the water and they turn into a boat. As you would expect, these vehicles are quite expensive. You probably wouldn't think of buying one for ordinary daily use, would you? How impractical! The truth is these amphibious vehicles are unwieldy; they make lousy cars and lousy boats. If you wanted to buy a boat, you would buy a boat. If you wanted a car, you would just go out and buy a car. Similarly, there is a similar problem in investing: Many people try to make all of their assets do everything at once. Like amphibious automobiles, we can all benefit from bearing in mind that it is more about deploying a portion of our assets to cover each area we need, not everything all at once.

This concept of practical, logical investing is really at the core of The Purpose-Based Retirement. This commonsense allows us to analyze different products across the board for what they really are. When we stop trying to put all of our eggs in one impossible basket, we are empowered to make more confident decisions.

This focus on solving for each liability of our retirement systematically also allows us to bypass some of today's current economic obstacles to retirement, such as record low interest rates and nosebleed stock-market valuations. There has never been a more prudent time to find the most efficient way to solve each of our retirement risks than today, instead of looking for the silver bullet to solve all your retirement woes.

From liquidity for emergencies and income to last a lifetime to growth for inflation protection and estate planning for our legacies, once we identify the emphasis and dollars needed to be allocated to each of these risks, we can find the most efficient investment vehicles to utilize to get us from point A to point B. Instead, most retirees find themselves jumping from one investment vehicle to the next and one financial advisor to the next looking for the one investment vehicle to solve all of their risks, be that mutual funds, annuities, life insurance, stocks, bonds, etc.

There is no perfect financial vehicle and there is no such thing as a bad investment — it simply depends on the PURPOSE we are trying to solve for.

Once we refocus on the liabilities we are trying to solve rather than fixating on the sum total of our assets, we began isolating and solving concerns systematically, so we can get money off our minds and focus on the real purpose of retirement: "Return on Life." It is my sincere hope that the suggestions presented here help you along your way to *your* Purpose-Based Retirement.

Casey Weade is a sought-after retirement planning professional, author of *Job Optional**, speaker, and CEO/Chief Visionary of the national financial firm, Howard Bailey. He hosts the "Retire with Purpose" radio, TV show, and podcast—providing sound financial guidance to pre-retirees and retirees across the country. He is also a member of the Forbes Finance Council and is a CERTIFIED FINANCIAL PLANNER™ (CFP®), Chartered Life Underwriter (CLU ®), Retirement Income Certified Professional® (RICP®), an Investment Advisor Representative, and holds licenses in life, accident, and health insurance.

Casey is not only passionate about guiding people toward a financially secure retirement, but he also zones in on what your golden years might look like. How will you spend your time? What will make you feel fulfilled? These questions are often left out of retirement planning, but Casey keeps them at the forefront. His ""Purpose-Based Retirement"" philosophy begins with finding your "why" and building a plan to protect that. In Casey's words, "The path to retirement is all about utilizing offensive strategies. But once you actually get there, the game switches to defending your purpose for retirement, and in turn your life savings from the major risks it will face."

While committed to helping as many retirees and pre-retirees as possible make smart financial decisions at a national level, Casey is also a lifelong Midwest native, and currently resides in Fort Wayne, Indiana, with his wife and two sons. He sponsors the Howard Bailey Junior Golf Tour as part of the Indiana Golf Foundation, and continues to stay active in his own community by supporting small businesses, local organizations, and charities throughout the year.

Contact Howard Bailey Financial™

Telephone: (866) 482-9559
Email: info@howardbailey.com
Website: www.howardbailey.com.

35387364R00062

Made in the USA
Middletown, DE
10 February 2019